# RECRUIT AND RETAIN THE BEST

# Books by John McCarter & Ray Schreyer

*Employer's Guide to Recruiting on the Internet*
*Recruit and Retain the Best*
*The Best 100 Web Sites for HR Professionals*

# Also in the CAREERSAVVY Series™:

*Anger and Conflict in the Workplace*
*100 Top Internet Job Sites*
*101 Hiring Mistakes Employers Make*
*The 100 Best Web Sites for HR Professionals*
*The Difficult Hire*
*Savvy Interviewing*
*The Savvy Resume Writer*

# Recruit and Retain the Best

John McCarter & Ray Schreyer

**IMPACT PUBLICATIONS**
Manassas Park, Virginia

### Library of Congress Cataloging-in-Publication Data

McCarter, John—
    Recruit and retain the best: key solutions for the HR professional / John McCarter & Ray Schreyer.
        p. cm.
      Includes index.
      ISBN 1-57023-134-6 (alk. paper)
        1. Employees—Recruiting—United States. 2. Employee retention—United States. I. Schreyer, Ray. II. Title.

HF5549.5.R44 S2953 2000
658.3'111—dc21

                                                                99-089878

**Publisher:** For information on Impact Publications, including current and forthcoming publications, authors, press kits, bookstore, and submission requirements, visit Impact's Web site: *www.impactpublications.com*

**Publicity/Rights:** For information on publicity, author interviews, and subsidiary rights, contact the Public Relations and Marketing Department: Tel. 703/361-7300 or Fax 703/335-9486.

**Sales/Distribution:** Bookstore sales are handled through Impact's trade distributor: National Book Network, 15200 NBN Way, Blue Ridge Summit, PA 17214, Tel. 1-800-462-6420. All other sales and distribution inquiries should be directed to the publisher: IMPACT PUBLICATIONS, 9104 Manassas Dr., Suite N, Manassas Park, VA 20111-5211, Tel. 703/361-7300, Fax 703/335-9486, or *careersavvy@impactpublications.com*

Book design by Kristina Ackley
Layout by Stacy Noyes

# Contents

# ACKNOWLEDGEMENTS

## John McCarter

This is a special acknowledgement to the students, team members, and coaches who have worked with me during the past twenty-two years of consulting to improve productivity, to develop training programs, to define work responsibilities, and in general to develop a continuing passion for human growth and achievement. I often learned more than I taught and I shared as much as I could with others. Some contributed more than others, but naming them would short change the energy and imagination of them all. To list only a very few of several thousand would take too much credit away from the earnest efforts of the others.

But a special thanks must go to my wife, Sue, whose challenging work with the autistic in North Carolina is a continuing source of inspiration. She brings her incredible patience home and humors my ongoing efforts to capture my experience in writing. Her insights are always incisive and her perspectives on human accomplishments are more generous than my own.

## Ray Schreyer

I would first like to thank my wife Gayle for allowing me to once again go off on the journey of writing a book. Hopefully this time I was able to find a better balance between this project and other pursuits. I will always cherish your constant love and support.

A great thanks to my friends and colleagues at Little & Associates. I am blessed to be working around some of the most fertile minds and creative spirits on this earth. Additionally, I am privileged to be among some of the most talented, dedicated, and fun HR professionals. Thanks Grace, Tanya, Susan, Rebekkah, Linda, and Kristen. I will forever cherish our friendships and working relationship.

Once again I wish to thank my partner in crime John McCarter. I can't believe we are doing this again. I think we have both learned the lesson: never say never.

# RECRUIT AND RETAIN THE BEST

# Introduction

This book has two objectives. The first is to consolidate the best of our experience on the issues and techniques involved. We are certain that our efforts have parallels in the work of many others, but we have organized our thoughts in a pattern that complements our second objective and we hope that the concise statements will be a format for action and introspection.

The second objective is to define and to celebrate a dynamic and irresistible trend in human resources—the talent powered company. Good companies and organizations have always recognized the importance of having competent, responsible, and well led employees. But changes in technology and society are now driving many to the realization that as an operating principle and strategic imperative, the acquisition and retention of highly quality staff is without peer.

Reengineering has painful limits, long term planning is frequently futile, and the best new software often becomes outdated before it is fully implemented. The soundest approach in a dynamic management environment is to identify, hire, inspire, and retain a diverse and able staff who can work together to handle all the varied uncertainties. Leadership is not a dead issue; we just need more of it at all levels and in the hands of people who do as well as direct.

The talent powered company is the new paradigm. This book is a rough outline of the concept; the actual definition is being written by the companies who have been too busy building talent powered companies to analyze their actions. They know what works and they enjoy the results.

# 1

## DEFINING THE BEST FOR THE
## TALENT POWERED ORGANIZATION

The biggest challenge faced by most organizations is defining the best in human resources. Before we attempt to enter the labor market and try to find and attract new employees, we must understand the complete profiles of the individuals we need to hire. Among the manifold and complicated process of recruiting, this is where most organizations make their most frequent and biggest mistakes!

They look for individuals who possess qualities that on the surface appear to define success: a good interview, excellent appearance, degree from the right school, etc., but often fall short in recognizing and measuring a number of more defining prerequisites for success in their organization. Most often that error is a product of either a faulty vision of the company's future or a short-range perspective of its place in the economy. If our planning is deficient, we can have a staff that is eminently qualified to perform tasks that are not cost effective to perform or no longer in demand. Even if our forecasting is precise, the accelerating pace of change makes any short planning window ripe with the same risks. The pivotal challenge is to select that elite minority that can provide outstanding results today and that can adapt to the repeated tides of change.

Intrinsic in those criteria are two important qualifiers—the persons we hire must be partial to a dynamic environment and there should be a mutual commitment for the long term growth of both the individuals selected and the organization. To find the first, we must examine the life and work history for performance vitality in the face of change. The second is more complicated, because it incorporates the concept that employees provide a special kind of security for their employer; that their commitment to corporate success generates a high degree of flexibility and innovation; and that the employee has the kind of personal energy required. There is a new playing field, requiring that management be willing to provide training, fair compensation, job security, and growth opportunities in return for the vital resource of employee loyalty.

But just what is "The Best?" We define it as the top 20% of the workers in any given job or occupation. Recent research has shown that the top 20% of employees account for 19% - 150% more productivity than the average of the next 80%. In other words, the top 20 percent produce more profits, work both harder and smarter, and contribute significantly to your bottom line. These are the key individuals whom you need in order to flourish in today's highly competitive environment. But the question remains, how do we define top employees? What do they possess which makes them different from the rest?

> ★ The top 20 percent produce more profits, work both harder and smarter, and contribute significantly to your bottom line. ★

## Selecting the Best

One of the major requirements of supervisory and management personnel is to select new employees. This "duty" is regarded by most as the bane of management actions. So much is riding on a decision. Often it takes a new employee weeks to learn the new systems, familiarize themselves with the organization, and move into a productive mode. Additionally, training and loss of productivity during the initial stages of their employment will cost the organization thousands of dollars. Heaven help the manager if the new hire fails in the job or decides to leave in the first few weeks of employment. No wonder such concerns give management headaches and insomnia!

Where we as managers often fail is in the criteria we use to select new talent for our staff. Consider what kinds of measures we typically use as a means of selection:

| | |
|---|---|
| Intelligence | College Degrees |
| Grades | References |
| Appearance | Knowledge |
| Gregariousness | Skills |
| Proximity to Job | Personality |

These criteria can be valid predictors of success on a job. But we all know about the genius who lacks social interaction skills, or the college dropout who rose to extreme business success—Bill Gates to name one. How about the individual with perfect appearance, but who can't spell, add or subtract? Better yet is the perfect interviewee—an individual who is a master of presentation, at selling themselves, at answering all of our questions correctly on what they would do in every situation. Sometimes their initial interview is the high point of their career at your company followed by a precipitous downhill slide from that moment on.

Talent powered organizations understand that superior performance is found in a person's competencies. To find the best we must first understand how to recognize the competencies that define superior performance for the job or position in question.

# Competency Defined

So what is a competency? It is an underlying characteristic of an individual that is found to predict success or excellent performance in a job, career, or situation. Competencies can be categorized into five different underlying characteristics:

1. **Motives**—These are the factors which drive an individual to action. They are the ideas, wants, and desires that are intrinsic and pivotal to individual performance. Motives govern the kinds of choices we make and the quantity of energy we invest in those choices. The entrepreneur who desires to retire a millionaire or the politician who craves to rise to State Representative possess strong and powerful motives which drive them to action and govern their choices and behavior. Others may simply want recognition as being the best at what they do, but the achievers who desire growth and success, however they define it, will make a significant impact as they strive to achieve their goals.

2. **Traits**—These are the ways we consistently respond to a given situation and the physical attributes we bring to the table. The manager who consistently responds to a crisis situation in a cool and composed manner or the baseball pitcher who consistently throws 90+ mile per hour fastballs are displaying traits. Traits are a combination of instinct, abilities, and experience that has matured into a pattern for action. They are successful adaptations to an environment. However, in a distinctively different environment, well-established and once attractive traits may be inappropriate or even counter-productive.

3. **Self-image**—Represents a person's attitudes, values, and morals. Self-image is the yardstick that people use to measure themselves. It sets boundaries on achievement and behaviors, either positive or negative. Self-image is the picture we see in the mirror when we are thinking about ourselves more than we are looking objectively at the image before us. Self-imagine can energize or retard the development of other competencies. Persons can take on new tasks and even new job roles with ease if the new responsibilities do not require major shifts in how they see themselves. People can stretch to meet new challenges, but real changes in personality are only slightly less likely than changes in their DNA.

4. **Knowledge**—What an individual knows about a subject area. Knowledge is an accumulation of facts and insights that a person has available for immediate application. Knowledge is gleaned through years of formal and informal study, and thoughtful experience. Any knowledge handicap must be evaluated in the light of a person's intellectual ability, their learning motivation, and the amount of time required mastering any new knowledge. The most complex aspect of the knowledge component is understanding what level of data and understanding is actually required. Sometimes the advanced degrees and the insights they claim are superfluous to career performance in both the open position and their long-term success with the employer.

5. **Skill**—Specific abilities to perform certain mental or physical tasks. Skills define the potential to produce outcomes without additional education or training. Driving a car,

typing a letter on a computer, or hitting a baseball are all examples of skills that require focused and repeated performances to incorporate into our collection of abilities. Skills are typically easier to demonstrate than to define. Increasingly job candidates are called upon to include in their portfolio of experience and competence a hard copy or software documentation of their proficiencies.

Traditionally organizations have relied on the latter two characteristics, knowledge and skills, to predict success in a given employment situation. Unfortunately, these two characteristics generally fail to accurately predict performance because it is difficult to actually assess how they will be used on the job. Rather, it is more important to understand the motives, traits, and self-concept that drive the behavior of the individual in question.

## Specific Competencies

Now that we have explored what makes up a competency, we can examine some specific competencies that define success in employment situations. Here are a few examples (with definitions) that are often used by employers:

- **Compassion**—Cares about others; is concerned about their problems; is sympathetic towards the less fortunate; has true empathy when someone is in pain. *A social worker may spend 6 years in college to gain a master's degree, may pass the state boards, and may land a job in a state agency, but he/she will not be effective or successful if he/she lacks compassion. All the knowledge and eloquence that a sales or customer service person can demonstrate may be futile without some empathy with the concerns of customers.*

- **Creativity**—Has new and unique ideas, excels at brainstorming solutions to problems, defines connections between unrelated concepts to form unique paths to success. *A graphic artist might be schooled in the latest versions of Pagemaker, Photoshop, and PowerPoint, but true successful presentations will be defined by the artist's creative flair more that the technical skills necessary to operate those software programs. Creativity is a tricky combination of intellectual flexibility and the self-esteem to defend and assert the products of their imaginations.*

- **Achievement Orientation**—Has specific focus on tasks at hand, desires to do the job well and achieve a standard of excellence. Sets himself/herself challenging goals and is driven to improve on these goals. Will take calculated risks and persist in the face of adversity. *Everyone knows such a driven individual, they are the leaders, the doers, the achievers. One basis for their success is a firmly entrenched achievement oriented competency.*

- **Teamwork**—Desires to share information and cooperate with others, expresses positive feelings to others in the workgroup, asks for others' help and input, publicly celebrates success of others, helps to further build cohesive workgroup. *The complex nature of today's work environment has made it imperative that individuals practice teamwork. The genius knowledge worker is of limited use to anyone if he/she can not clearly work with and through others by gaining their acceptance, respect, and trust. It all starts and ends with teamwork.*

The following is a listing of several competencies currently being used to select folks at talent powered companies worldwide. See if some of the following words describe the basis of talent and performance amongst your current staff:

| | |
|---|---|
| Achievement Oriented | Initiative |
| Analytical Thinker | Information Seeking |
| Business Savvy | Intellectual Ability |
| Commitment | Leadership |
| Compassion | Perseverance |
| Concern for Quality | Presentation Skills |
| Confidence | Relationship Builder |
| Customer Service Oriented | Teamwork |
| Delegation | Team Leadership |
| Flexibility | Written Communications |

The top 20% are an elite group and can be expensive resources. They become cost effective when their career objectives and competencies correspond to organizational goals, and their management leaders guide effective implementation. The best, however, do more than perform. They also grow. The special challenges that talent powered organizations accept is the timely fostering and exercise of that growth.

## Defining a Specific Model

The following competencies are those most associated with success as a manager. Consider how many organizations promote individuals to the management ranks: they select the individual who is the most loyal, hardest working, and most technically proficient. They give him or her a 2-4 day training class in "How to Manage" and a pep talk from upper management. Next we have the final step: this new leader, fresh from the training course and pep talk are "let loose" on the workforce. Everyone hopes for the best. Unfortunately, hope does not translate into performance. No wonder there is a high level of failure when this tactic is employed. It is far better to select for the appropriate individual: one who possesses the basic competencies to succeed in the job!

Let us now consider what exactly is needed to be successful as a manager. One of the primary needs of a manager is to have the ability to develop his or her employees: to be a teacher, trainer, and coach; to provide realistic feedback on performance; and to provide support. Another aspect of successful management is to have the ability to be a leader: to use positional power effectively; to take charge and act decisively; to enforce standards of quality and discipline. Finally, a successful manager must be able to engender a sense of teamwork and camaraderie in their staff: must effectively build group relationships; work to maintain harmony and resolve conflict; motivate members of the team.

Let's take a closer look at these three managerial competencies:

## Developing Subordinates

Key Attributes:
- Maintains positive expectations of members of his/her workgroup
- Provides instructions, demonstrations, positive role modeling
- Provides staff developmental feedback to aid in growth/learning
- Provides encouragement and support
- Provides long term development and strategic training
- Has awareness towards new staff developmental needs
- Delegates appropriately to have staff try out new skills
- Promotes staff when skills are mastered

## Leadership

Key Attributes:
- Keeps staff informed of events
- Holds staff meetings to discuss business issues
- Manages team effectiveness and morale
- Takes charge of the staff
- Gains respect as leader from the team
- Defines a team vision and purpose
- Maintains standards of quality

## Teamwork

Key Attributes:
- Shares information and cooperates with others.
- Solicits input from others on team
- Empowers others to act
- Promotes team harmony
- Resolves conflicts among group members

Once we have defined a series of competencies for a position, the placement of individuals into that position becomes much clearer. For existing staff, where performance data is already evident, it should be readily apparent if the internal candidate has "the right stuff" to succeed in the new position. For selection of new staff, your seasoned HR professionals should be able to provide you with the selection tools necessary to screen for these attributes.

> ★
> Once we have defined a series of competencies for a position, the placement of individuals into that position becomes much clearer.
> ★

## Moving Forward

Our goal in this chapter was to "whet your appetite" and help you understand the new way of defining talent within organizations. No longer will it be based on degrees, certification, or years of service. Rather it is being defined today by talent powered organizations as the competencies possessed by the workforce. Your challenge, as a supervisor, manager, or organization leader, is to meet with your Human Resources Department and work with them to develop competency models for your organization. Once you have defined exactly which competencies are necessary for successful performance, your HR staff can define and refine selection systems, performance management tools, compensation plans, and development systems based on the custom collected criteria for successful performance.

One of the important insights that we hope you will gain from this book is that even though the process of hiring and retaining top talent is a complex and demanding endeavor, the successful accomplishment has great and proven potential for minimizing the other difficulties that burden and harass management. With a competent and well-motivated staff doing the work and developing new opportunities for the company, the balance of a manager's responsibilities take on a new perspective. By managing this crucial task well, the balance of a manager's duties can simply be described as leadership. That is the simple secret of a talent powered company.

# 2

# THE LOOMING TALENT WARS

I f your organization does not feel the impact of the looming talent wars today, you will in the coming decade. This nation is entering a period of constrained human resources that has been unparalleled since our founding. Partly a product of happenstance (World War II), partly by our inadequate training systems, and partly by the information age, we are entering a time where talent is becoming a scarce resource. In a nation where almost everyone has acquired the same access to computers, systems, and technologies, organizations are finding more and more that the main distinction between them and their competitors is their ability to find, attract, and retain top talent.

## The Talent Concept

If you are a professional with a few years of experience, human resources are taking on a new meaning in the English lexicon. The concept most of us have identified with has been the word labor — which is defined by most as the raw, brute force and basic mechanical skills which can be hired to do a job. In the last century and most of this one, labor was hired to work on the farm, to assemble pieces of a automobiles on a moving line, to drive a fork lift delivering supplies on a factory floor, or to weigh and pour chemicals into a reactor at a polymer factory. Labor was often easily available at a reasonable price since the accent was on strength, dexterity, and loyalty instead of the type of competencies that are necessary in the information age.

But the world has progressed, jobs have evolved, and the nation has passed from a rural farming economy, to a manufacturing economy, and now, to the dawn of the information economy. Raw, brute, force and basic mechanical skills are seldom needed to fuel the engine of our new age. Our technology has evolved from massive steam engines to an energy network with huge electric generators at one end and everything from powerful engines to tiny servomotors at the other. Energy has become cheap and portable, thousands of simple skills have been captured in silicon chips.

Now the critical resource is the accumulation of special knowledge, skills, abilities and competencies. They drive the creation of new businesses and foster the creative energies to compete in the information age. The challenging need today is to find, attract, and retain talent. Once a few good managers, a sound business plan, capital, and a loyal staff could almost guarantee success. They are still in great demand and too often unappreciated as well. But the requirements have been ratcheted up and there is a much more wide spread need for strong preparation and professionalism at every level. Whether we call them knowledge workers or mini-managers, our organizations demand a strong combination of learning, practical experience, responsibility, and initiative in everyone we hire.

Talent is now the lifeblood of the organization, because only by having a talent-laden organization will a company be able to move at a moment's notice when presented by the fast-paced challenges of the information age. Product life cycles are shortening, technological obsolescence often takes place before the equipment is fully depreciated, the Internet has expanded the average person's general knowledge base exponentially, economic rules are being broken faster than they are established, instant polls assess what people are think-

ing, computer networks track what we are
doing, and we are often overwhelmed by
the sheer volume of decisions that must
be made. The organizations that continue
to thrive in this environment will be dis-
tinguished by their ability to hire and retain people who have the skills and intel-
lect to prevail.

> ★
> Our organizations
> demand a strong
> combination of
> learning, practical
> experience, responsi-
> bility, and initiative
> in everyone we hire.
> ★

The picture for future employment trends is by no means rosy.
According to a recent survey in the information technology profession there were approximately 350,000 unfilled information technology jobs in America at the beginning of 1999. In addition, the
Commerce Department has projected that by the year 2006, America
will need over 1.3 million new highly skilled information technology
specialists to include software engineers and architects, programmers, and system analysts.

But it is not just the IT arena that is affected. Recent headlines in
leading newspapers and periodicals paint an equally disturbing picture for talent at all levels:

- "Staff Shortage Called Acute in Long-Term Care"

- "Michigan Sugar Processors Facing Bumper Crop, Worker
  Shortage"

- "Maine in Grip of Worker Shortage—Some Companies
  are Paying Finders' Fees to Get New Workers Into the Fold,
  While Others Scout the World"

- "Worker Shortage Could Threaten Drilling Rebound"

- "Automakers Face Worker Shortage"

- "Workplace Challenge of 21st Century—Learning Technology Skills"

■ "20/20 Exposes Shortages in Training of EMS Personnel Answering 911 Calls"

Times have truly changed, and all organizations that desire to have long term impact on their industry in the next century must focus on talent issues. The good ideas in hiring are becoming urgent. Your organization must take a proactive stance on this issue or greatly risk becoming a footnote in business history.

## The Boomers Go Bust

Two unprecedented world events set the stage for part of our current talent dilemma. In the 30's America was mired in a major depression that underutilized human and capital resources to the point that growth nearly halted. In the 40's a major war in Europe forced America to stretch itself to the limits in its resources. For nearly 15 years the country experienced extreme hardship and sacrifice.

But all changed in the mid 40's with the ending of World War II. With Europe in ruins and America relatively unscathed, we entered a growth period unprecedented in our history. The returning troops went to college on the G.I. bill, helped industry switch from war time munitions to production of both consumer and capital goods, built millions of homes for the growing families, and used their skills and experience to build a completely new infrastructure of business and commerce. They also started the baby boom generation.

Now in the 1990's those boomers, who represent a giant spike in terms of population, are beginning to turn gray and opt for retirement. But who exactly is left to replace them? By the year 2015 it is estimated that there will be approximately 15% fewer Americans in the important 35 to 45 year-old age range. At the same time the economy is expected to continue growing at a robust rate, and the expectations of the boomers for a government-assisted retirement emphasize the need for continued economic growth. We are facing a major shortage in human capital.

## Enter Our Education System

While the supply of youth will shrink in the next few decades, the resources and programs to train and develop those individuals has stagnated. Consider some major challenges faced by our education system:

- We have installed billions of dollars worth of computer hardware into the nation's classrooms, and left most of the teachers to acquire the relevant skills on their own while simultaneously teaching the students. And many of those teachers managed to avoid information age skills in both their general undergraduate studies and formal education preparation.

- Although less than 2% of our population is involved in agricultural pursuits, we cling to a nine months out of the year educational calendar designed to make children available to work the fields in the summer. We continue to build school buildings without air conditioning because the students will not be there in the summer, locking us into historical patterns.

- The most telling results of the past generation in national education is the rapid growth and desperate popularity of home schooling. When families that are capable of conducting home schooling will forgo the almost standard second income to rescue their children from the public school system, alarms should go off across the nation. Private schools are also growing, at a rate that almost matches the increased tuition they charge.

■ In some school systems, there is more growth in security equipment and personnel than there is in textbook purchases. Students in even the best public schools often share textbooks of dubious quality.

The object of this extended litany of educational problems is to emphasize that employers will be facing ever-increasing competition for scarce, high quality human resources. They will cost more, be more difficult to find, and challenging to retain. Those employers who are not prepared to innovate and beat the odds will find themselves handicapped in the performance of critical organizational functions. "Timid recruiters" is an oxymoron. "Complacent human resource professionals" are obsolete.

> ★ The advent of new technologies and business processes has eliminated thousands of once lucrative careers leaving a nation with millions of senior/retired workers minus the necessary skills to compete in the new age. ★

To further complicate the situation, a majority of the next generation of high school students will have felt the pain, directly or indirectly, of a business downsizing or re-engineering or old-fashioned layoff, or of having parents switch jobs to achieve advancement they couldn't obtain at their current job. With the one job career becoming a historical anomaly instead of a community standard, the young recruits of the future will present distinctive new challenges.

## A New Era

But it is getting worse. The advent of the information age is creating a major paradigm shift in how we think, act, and conduct our businesses. Gone are the pencil, pen, and typewriter. Enter the PC, email, and the laser printer. The advent of new technologies and business processes has eliminated thousands of once lucrative careers leaving a nation with millions of senior /retired workers minus the necessary skills to compete in the new age. Even middle-age workers are being challenged to learn the new technologies, which change on a weekly basis, while trying to raise a family and accumulate their piece of the American dream.

The labor market continues to be haunted by 19th century concepts about the nature and source of wealth. When Adam Smith wrote his pivotal book that featured a dramatic example of how the expense of hiring craftsmen could be avoided by having a series of unskilled workers complete the various steps involved in manufacturing pins, he laid the foundations of the industrial revolution. But the innovations that made mass production an economic miracle is now a nightmare for the information age, its knowledge workers, and the companies who need them.

Most of the Adam Smith type jobs have been mechanized and automated, and you can't find the staff on the street corner to manufacture, repair, program, and maintain those high technology wonders.. But the thought process that considers employees to be as interchangeable as the components in a machine prevails. Despite all the evidence to the contrary, management clings to a bias that the bell curve of employee ability is flat. We take excellence in athletic and dramatic ability for granted, but turn a blind eye to the differences in the contribution of those that add value in industry, business, and commerce.

The results have broad implications:

- The quality of training and education provided employees is often marginal. Stingy funding is reinforced by an attitude that turnover is inevitable, and companies are often overwhelmed by the gaps in new hire education left by the various schools and colleges. A chicken or egg issue has developed regarding the risks of training and the associated costs. Companies do not want the expense of training staff wasted when they leave and go to work for someone else. They use their political clout to starve the public educational system, and they expect that employees will come to them in large numbers and be ready to be productive the first week (minimum).

- A bias toward low base wages and salaries make employee initiative for individual development an equally risky proposition. As companies back away from the concept of a one-employer career, there are fewer stated or implied promises to encourage personal development. If there is not an obvious career path for advancement, employee planned training is perceived as a precursor of a job change, not typically regarded as either good news or proof of loyalty.

- Many wage and salary administration plans rob managers of the ability to successfully award excellent performance. They are precluded from being competitive irrespective of their unit's income per employee or other performance criteria. Employees must find a job elsewhere, or threaten to leave in order to get a decent raise.

- Across the board, cost of living raises address dire needs, but are a not-so-subtle insult to outstanding and excellent performers. They indicate a management lack of concern and profound laziness in the skills that justify management compensation. What are the hourly employees to think when managers take the easy way out?

- The continuing clamor for limiting the minimum wage and promotion of other restrictive barriers to a competitive labor market are becoming more apparent to employees and the public at large. The importation of thousands of foreign nationals to perform IT work that is often trumpeted to be the fuel of our economic growth is a legitimate source of concern. On one hand the national minimum wage is held to $5.15 an hour because companies cannot afford to pay more for the services those citizens provide, but we are unable to educate and train them for more productive jobs. National policy encourages legal and illegal immigration from Latin America to fill low wage jobs, and maintains a special program to bring in systems analysts, programmers, and other IT professionals to fill high tech jobs at relatively bargain prices.

## Talent Wars

The signs on the road ahead all point to an all out war for talent in the next several decades. We have seen the first major battles in the war begun in the Information technology arena. Organizations are left scarred on a daily basis as headhunters continually call into IT departments and use every trick in the book to lure away your organizational stars. In time, it will spread to other industries as the supply of talent becomes more and more scarce. It is time for you and your organization to begin asking the tough questions and to start preparing for the rocky road ahead:

1. Does your organization currently understand the challenges that lie ahead?
2. Are you willing to pull out all the stops to find and attract the best?
3. Will you consider changes in your whole organization and compensation structure to keep the best?

4. Have you examined the competencies, tenure, and longevity of current employees to evaluate current status and recent trends?

5. Are you confident that the pipeline that has brought good people to you in the past will be able to meet your needs for the immediate future?

6. Is long term planning for human resource needs on the agenda for senior management review and action?

7. Does your management have the courage and insights to lead a talent powered company?

# 3

# KEY CORPORATE BUILDING BLOCKS

Excellent employee retention efforts must be built upon a solid foundation. Later in the book we discuss specific strategies to enhance your recruiting and retention efforts. We begin here, however, by discussing the "Key Corporate Building Blocks" which serve as a base for successful recruiting and retention efforts. While specific individual strategies to find and keep employees may fill short term goals and needs, it is the building blocks, when present and in full use, that add to long term recruiting and retention success within your organization and/or workgroup. As might be expected these building blocks are not something that can be put in place overnight, nor are they quick fixes to your retention woes, rather they are the solid components of a well run business and may take years to develop.

We present the ten key building blocks that serve as the foundation for building a talent powered company:

## Workplace as a System

Top organizations and managers understand that every action, whether it is a quiet chat in the hallway to a new employee or an email to "all employees" about company phone usage policy, has an impact. Systems thinking involves understanding the phrase, "every action has an equal and opposite reaction." A manager who prac-

24

tices systems thinking sees the organization as an ecology of forces: formal and informal cultures; policies; strategies; decision making patterns; power systems; formal value systems; communication patterns. She understands that every action, every comment, even inaction communicates a message to the workforce. Because of this she has learned to become adept at understanding the nuisance of language, comments, actions and even in-actions.

Consider how the following may have an effect on an organization:

- The CEO of a large bank lavishes praise on the capital markets division as the savior of the organization. Employees hear this news and begin a mass migration to this new division as positions become available. Other areas in the institution are left in dire need for talent from the transfers.

- An engineering firm develops a compensation structure that heavily rewards managers based on the profits of their specific workgroup. By year-end employees are pushed into working 60+ hours per week by overeager, compensation driven managers. Burnout among the staff is evident, and turnover becomes rampant.

- Strand Associates has a bonus aystem for "Key Staff Employees." Individuals on this program are compensated for being "Key and Vital to the Success of the Organization." While the program is a major incentive to those few employees who are considered important, can you guess the reaction by employees who are not "key and vital" to the success of the organization?

In all the cases cited, the organization was attempting to achieve a positive outcome. By lavishing praise, the CEO of the bank wanted to motivate the new Capital Markets group, the engineering firm wanted managers to care about profits, and Strand Associates desired to further reward "Key Employees."

Yet all the actions had unintended negative consequences with immediate and long-term effects. The CEO of the bank alienated key managers in other divisions with such comments. The push for profits at the engineering firm delivered a short term gain in profits, but the loss of employees due to overwork destroyed the firms ability to retain talent in the market and thus doomed their future success. Strand Associates' "Key Staff Plan" created a furor just because of the wording of the name.

## Ethics, Integrity, Honesty, and Trust

Ethics, integrity, honesty, and trust form the core of any enterprise that is successful in attracting and especially retaining talented leaders. Would any company hire a person who does not adhere to standard business ethics, who lacks integrity of action, and who is dishonest? Should an intelligent, talented individual consider a long-term career with a company that displayed the same shortcomings? If you take the job and learn later that you cannot trust your employer, is there any reason to stay? The best employees understand the phrase, "but for the grace of God go I." Organizations that conduct their business affairs in an unethical, dishonest manner will attract similar type employees—but not the best.

> ★
> Ethics, integrity, honesty, and trust form the core of any enterprise that is successful in attracting and especially retaining talented leaders.
> ★

Companies who place a high value on such virtues will have the distinct advantage in the talent acquisition and retention wars! The careless tolerance once displayed for corporate mischief is finally waning with the realization that unbridled preoccupation with profits and growth can have direct negative impacts on employees, customers, the environment, and the society as a whole.

Does your organization:

- Conduct business according to professional standards and practices?

- Does your company culture support disclosure of the truth even when it hurts?

- Do members of your organization follow through on commitments and promises?

- If a major mistake or business catastrophe occurs, will your management team accept responsibility and act accordingly to rectify the situation? Or will your culture support cover-up or deflection of blame?

- Do you mention and endorse positive virtues in your company mission and vision statements?

- Are employees rewarded who live by such virtues and conversely, employees who stray from them punished?

- Do stories circulate within the company celebrating how a colleague cut corners and became an overnight success? Are laws, regulations, and industry standards evaded as well as observed?

- Has the CEO and other top management staff earned the trust of the workforce?

If your organization fails in these virtues, it is time to do some serious soul searching and take decisive action to repair the damage. Lack of ethics, integrity, honesty and trust is a cancer that spreads within the culture and gradually erodes the morale of the workforce.

## Organizational Feedback Loops

In most organizations information flows in one direction—down. The CEO makes the decisions, passes orders to the division presidents who in turn develop game plans with their vice-presidents, and so on and so forth. Successful organizations understand both the value and the need to stay in touch with the moods, feelings, and opinions of the workforce. Everyone thinks, has opinions, and desires to give feedback to management. Making an intellectual investment in the success of an employer is another kind of ownership; being concerned about its operations broadens involvement and commitment.

*Early in my career I was employed by a large chemical manufacturer. The division president was a master of understanding the importance of using organizational feedback. On his monthly trips from Chicago to Charlotte, NC, he would arrive the evening before his scheduled meeting with the local plant brass. He would check into his hotel, change into jeans and a polo shirt, stop by the local Krispy Kreme donut shop and arrive at the plant with several dozen donuts in hand at the shift change. He would spend the next several hours walking the floors talking to employees and getting to know everyone. Within a few months he knew basically everyone in the workforce, had built extreme loyalty and respect amongst the workgroup, and effectively had a check in place on the work of his managers. Whenever a problem or issue arose, the workforce knew that Nick was only one call or a visit away.*

If you want to increase your organizational feedback, here are seven things you should do:

1. Conduct annual or semi-annual company surveys, be as aggressive in collecting their inputs as you are in getting feedback from customers and clients. Employees are your critical customers; they know sooner if something is go-

ing wrong, can be a major ally in setting them straight, and have a vested interest in company success.

2. Spend time with your staff socially. Establish expectations for civil exchanges of information and concerns. Treat them with respect and regard.

3. Conduct weekly staff or organization wide meetings. Have an agenda that facilitates input and minimizes pontificating by management.

4. Ask for your staff's input. Routinely ask, "What do you think we should do about this?"

5. Have a suggestion box and/or a question board. Provide recognition of good suggestions and rapid responses to concerned questions. Don't be bashful about communicating.

6. Conduct exit interviews with all departing employees. Use the opportunity to get as much data as possible about the real reasons for the departure, and determine what kind of changes would be necessary to entice good employees to return. Ensure that the departing employee is confident in both the discretion and authority of the person conducting the interview.

7. Create an "answer board" on which any employee can post a question, signed or unsigned, to be answered on the board by the appropriate management authority within twenty-four hours.

## Putting People First

The decade of the 80's brought about massive changes and initiative in corporate America. It began with a small television program in 1982 called "If Japan Can, Why Can't We." With this program on

NBC, America was introduced to the concept of quality and the teachings of W. Edwards Demming. In time a culture of quality spread across America and the concept of "Customer Service" and "Customer Delight" became the zeitgeist of the 80's. But who creates this customer service, who creates the attitude, the spark, the desire for client to come back to your organization—IT IS YOUR PEOPLE.

*Big Company USA is a strong proponent of "Putting the Customer First" and doing anything to please their corporate clients. During the decade of the 90's they formed a corporate culture which thrived on "putting the client first". When clients made mistakes Big Company never corrected their clients; they corrected mistakes and did whatever the client needed. At the end of the decade the jury was in: the client still was not happy, and employees at Big Company were burnt out from putting in the expected 60+ hours per week. Turnover grew as did the number of employees who developed an "I don't care attitude."*

In the end it's all about your people. If they are motivated, are happy, incented properly, and are taken care of—you the employer and your clients will win. But if they feel abused, misunderstood, or treated wrongly—all bets are off for excellent customer service and support.

The talent shortage of the 90's has further complicated the problem. While the economy has been strong, businesses are often faced with the prospect of either:

- Turning down work due to lack of available talent, or
- Stretching their staff to complete the extra work.

Left with these choices, many businesses have opted to stretch their staff to the fullest. By example or work assignments, management precludes personal vacations, time off with family, training time, professional peer meetings, sports, and many social contacts. Such treatment begins a turnover cycle, which forces more pressure on available resources, which leads to more turnover. During the extended turnover process, two critical factors occur that are rarely noted:

1. The talent leaving the organization tends to be of high quality (excellent knowledge, skills, abilities, and competencies) and a thorough knowledge of client needs and company policies.
2. The talent entering the organization as replacement is rarely ever of the same caliber as those that just left, and represents a long learning curve and fractured relationships with the client/customer base.

The focus on employees first, then the customer, is truly a shift in thinking. But as we move from a manufacturing based economy (where quality systems protect customer from negative employee performance) to a service based economy (where the typical employee has major and immediate impact), the rules have begun to change. Certainly the client is still vitally important, and good customer service and management is still a major component of a successful business enterprise, but it can not come at the exclusion of excellent employee service and management.

Some critical questions are: If your employees were your customers, would the work environment, task leadership, and benefits administration be sufficient to retain them as customers? Would key customer people be pleased to work at your facilities? If a spouse, sibling, child, or personal friend of a key customer were to become employed at your company, would your reputation become enhanced or destroyed?

# Fairness

Fairness is a basic core principle that is universally ascribed to by almost all organizations. Just as safety and quality have become basic core corporate virtues, so has fairness. The challenge arises out of what is meant by the concept of fairness. Employees and management often differ on the definition. Employers tend to view fairness in the realm of access to opportunity—everyone has an equal shot to get rewards, promotions, and the other advantages of hard work and loyalty. Employees on the other hand view fairness in regard to outcomes—how many talented and productive individuals actually get promotions or raises.

*Doris was a minimalist. In her job as HR Director she understood her job simply—to find the best people as cheaply as possible. Isn't that what success is all about—gaining talent while keeping a tight watch on the bottom line? She did fine at first. She was able to source and hire individuals who were somewhat off market—maybe they had a bad experience with their former employer and just left in frustration, or maybe they did not understand their true market value. It didn't matter; Doris would promise the future and keep the current salary as low as possible.*

Doris was successful in her efforts of recruiting, but major issues developed with retention. As the situation for her recruits changed, and they found themselves not only below market, but also more appreciated in the talent marketplace, they sought out positions with more competitive packages. Doris had taken a narrow view of her job, to simply acquire talent at the lowest possible initial cost, rather than a long-term perspective of securing a person's services for the long term. Of course, the managers appreciated her bargain hunting—again and again. There is a shared responsibility between line managers and human resource recruiters to think in terms of extended service. The issue should not be how cheaply can I get this new employee, but rather it should be what is a fair salary for the job and what will it take to retain those services on *a long term basis.*

Do you and your organization treat everyone fairly?

- Are individuals rewarded based on the contributions they make to the organization—or are they rewarded as to the political pull they possess? Are decisions based on what is fair and just, or are they based on who has or who lacks power?
- Do all individuals at the same level have access to the same information, opportunities, and social interaction?
- Do the CEO and other senior managers give as much attention to women and minorities as they do to male staff members?
- Do all employees feel as if they are given a fair shake?

## Acceptance of Diversity

Does your organization accept diversity? As in:

- Diversity of opinion
- Diversity of background
- Diversity of size, shape, type, race, nationality
- Diversity of interest

Diversity is a key ingredient in assuring an organization has a wealth of talent and skills needed for our ever-changing culture.

But what is diversity? We define it as openness to including in the organization knowledge, skills, abilities, thoughts, actions, and styles different from the normative culture. It is the leading organizations that understand that these differences translate into significant and important organizational strengths and who celebrate them.

- Do company publications celebrate the various backgrounds that contribute to corporate diversity?

- Does your organization employ folks who do not fit the corporate mold and march to a different drummer?

- Does your company include bright people in its efforts to celebrate and encourage diversity?

- Does management consider diversity in the selection of work groups or special project teams?

- Are there calendars published that reflect the distinctively different holidays the work force celebrates? Are exceptions made to accommodate that diversity?

- Are there job functions within the company that obviously prize innovative persons? Are there others that reject any kind of imagination?

- If there is a company cafeteria, are menus developed that reflect some variety of backgrounds represented in the workforce?

Diversity is more than tolerance, it is the deliberate celebration of differences and distinctions. One of my favorite instructors begins classes with an extended introduction exercise called "Personal Best." Every participant is encouraged to describe something they have done that is a special source of pride, either work related or otherwise. By the end of these exchanges, the class has a heightened sense of individual values. Some members understand and accept colleagues twice

> Diversity is more than tolerance, it is the deliberate celebration of differences and distinctions.

as well as they did before—even though they have been working together for years.

Diversity is best promoted by its integration into the fabric of how an organization works.

## Openness

All people think. The best and the brightest, those who you want to attract and retain tend to think the most. They think about their jobs, their career, and their organization. They are learned, curious, and inquisitive. They desire to be part of an organization where opinions, thought, feedback, and truth are practiced. If you want them to stay and be part of your team you must have an organization which is open and inclusive.

Traditionally organizations have run with several levels of communication with each level being less than forthcoming in their openness and candor to the level below. The senior executive committee holds facts closely, such as financial and performance data and lets members of the management committee in on data on a need to know basis. In turn, managers only share information with line employees only when they deem it absolutely necessary. Such actions create an organization where the vast majority of the workforce has no idea about profitability and performance, and with which they thus have no stake or ownership.

No seasoned professional would want to stay with an organization that fails to provide meaningful and open information. Hiding information and snowing the workforce may have had success in past generations but such actions will truly stifle organizations in this information age.

Do you work for an open organization?

- Are employees given an opportunity to fully understand the organization, their place in it, and what it takes to achieve success?

- Do employees and management have the freedom to have frank and open dialogue with peers and leaders?

- Is financial data and competitive intelligence shared with the workforce and do they understand their place in it?

- Are operating policies clear, brief, and unambiguous?

## Fun Factor

Do folks in your organization laugh? Do workgroups sometimes cutup and have a good time together? Are there birthday parties and celebrations of success?—OR can you cut the tension with a knife? Let's face it, folks like to work and be around a fun and vibrant environment. When folks are having fun at their job, it stops being the dreaded work, and transitions into an energizing activity.

One of my recent employers represented a true example of the fun factor. The founder of the organization had the title "Master of Madness" and would often lead brainstorming sessions dressed in a Viking Hat replete with horns. Such lighthearted fare fueled a fun vibrant environment that fueled success and growth in the late 90's.

Here's how to have some fun in your organization:

- Take your entire staff to the local comedy club.

- Go out as a group to an amusement park.

- Tell jokes, be playful.

- Get rid of that suit and tie—relax.

- Personalize a birthday cake.

- Spotlight hobbies and interests of employees.

- Involve the company in the community.

## Employee Connectivity

It is human nature to have the desire to be part of something. That something can be a cause, an idea, a vision, or a purpose. Beyond the paycheck and general creature comforts of a comfortable work environment, folks want to be connected to an organization that expects the best they have to offer and rewards their accomplishment. Unless they are rigorously trained to be indifferent, people chose to work with a passion. Some examples are:

- The architect who lives in the design studio for two weeks straight pouring her soul into the design for the next library for the university.

- The NASA engineer who gave 110% on the Apollo program to "place a man on the moon by the end of the decade."

- The hospice worker who gains enormous satisfaction from providing counseling to the sick and dying.

These are examples of connectivity to a job or profession. Still on another level is connectivity is to a team or workgroup. Teams often become so tight that they play ball together, socialize together, and form lasting friendships. People seldom leave companies if their best friends and most rewarding experiences are associated with their employment. In terms of personal links, with the exception of live combat and sports participation, few associations are as strong as the bonds that commit the people who work together to one another.

> ★
> Connectivity is the most valuable asset an organization can have and it should never be underestimated.
> ★

But most importantly is connectivity to an employer. This is the most valuable asset an organization can have and it should never be underestimated. Organizations at the top of attracting and retaining employees have developed in their current workforce a bond that is unmatched. But such connectivity is not easily earned. It is the culmination of doing all the other nine factors well.

Just how important is connectivity—extremely. In our travels we have noticed dozens of situations of employee turnover due to connectivity issues. A good friend of mine who was Japanese-American and lived in San Francisco lasted one-year in Charlotte, NC due to "cultural issues." A former secretary I knew left her "Yankee" husband after one year of moving to Wisconsin—she wanted to be back home.

Another area of concern that can be divisive and lead to premature turnover is the existence of cliques within your organization. If some of your employees feel as if they are unable to gain membership in the appropriate workgroups or connect with the appropriate people your turnover statistics may continue to rise.

What can an organization or manager do regarding this issue? One solution is to spend time making sure all new employees find a social outlet within the organization and the community. As John Locke stated, "No man is an island." Everyone has the basic needs to connect with others.

## Viewing People Management as a Strategic Business Issue

We end where we basically need to begin, to understand that the most important imperative for your organization is to focus on the management of your people as a strategic business issue. Understanding that people are of vital concern drives organizational behavior towards employee training and development, ensuring fairness in compensation and benefits programs, and engenders a positive attitude in the minds of management and workers alike.

## Building on the Foundation

There are specific steps an organization can take to improve on several of the ten building blocks. Your corporate HR Department can help define the deficiency gaps between the desired state and the current state. We do suggest that you undertake at minimum a yearly assessment of the state and mood of the workforce. This should serve as an excellent starting point at determining the strength of your corporate priorities, but if there are significant gaps between the desired output and the current reality, major changes in corporate leadership may be the only solution.

### Steps to Improve On The Foundation

1. Consult with experienced HR professionals and Organizational Development experts on human relation issues within your workforce. Develop indices to track overall vitality of the company/employee relationship.
2. Stay in touch with your workforce by instituting weekly informational gatherings, company social gatherings, and conducting annual employee surveys.
3. Conduct frank discussions with exiting employees to determine gaps in your foundation.
4. Absolutely demand adherence and acceptance to a solid standard of values and conduct.
5. Begin using email and/or newsletters to begin informational communication with your workforce. Include a balance of both social and business information.

6. Have employee profiles in your newsletter and on your corporate Intranet site. Include information about the individuals, their interests, hobbies, etc.

7. Begin treating all employees as cherished business partners and key to your organization's success.

8. Stop being so serious—have some fun—get rid of that stodgy old corporate environment.

9. Energize a HR function that is dedicated towards sponsoring the social interaction needs of the workforce.

10. Perform an assessment of how well senior management is committed to being the kind of talent powered company that can succeed and prosper in the next millennium. Are they personally committed to the kinds of changes necessary or are they comfortable with the role of stumbling blocks?

11. In supervisor and other leadership training, incorporate techniques and expectations for serious involvement of supervisors and managers at every level to demonstrate and promote the company as a great place to be and grow.

Obviously, creating a talent powered organization requires more than hiring and retaining a better class of employees. It also demands that management deliberately fosters a culture whose participants grow as well as produce.

# 4

## Finding Talent

The first big hurdle to cross when presented with the challenge of finding additional staff is to determine exactly where to start. In this chapter we discuss several of the traditional and several non-traditional methods employers are now using to get in touch with prospective employees. With the economy in hyperdrive and the unemployment rate at an all time low, employers are resorting to all types of creative ways for connecting with future employees.

### Employee Referral

Without a doubt, employee referrals can be the absolute best way to find talent for your company. All of your most talented individuals have made dozens of friends and acquaintances in college, professional, and industry circles. Employee referrals represent the most cost effective way to recruit and place talented individuals within your organization. Employees take great care in making sure that the individuals they recommend are of high caliber and well suited for success within the organization. Anything less would definitely reflect badly on their reputation within the organization. Plus it often can be a badge of honor to be known as the one who helped build a solid work team. Such pre-qualification of talent will be music to any highly stressed recruiting staff.

The major challenges we find with referral programs is with intro-ducing the program to employees and keeping the excitement going towards production of good quality applicants. Programs often start with a bang via company newsletters, Intranet sites, and meetings. But in a short time a referral program can often get forgotten as employees transfer to other departments, change their current tasks, and generally forget. Efforts must be taken to regularly keep the program in front of all employees. Unless one is faced with a se-verely shrinking market, you should always be looking for outstand-ing staff.

## Tips on Implementing an Employee Referral Program

1. Start by deciding the scope of the program. Nothing works better than offering employees some type of reward for bringing a new employee on board. Rewards can be in the form of cash bonuses, gift certificates to the company store, mini-vacations, or tickets to a drawing for a yearly mega-prize like a BMW or Mercedes.

2. Once you have decided exactly what types of rewards are given for a successful hire, determine the process for submitting resumes (who gathers them) and criteria for award pay outs (how long must the candidate stay before the gift is given).

3. Develop communications brochures for employees that describe the program in detail along with instructions for resume submittal (email, paper, etc.)

4. Discuss the program in your new employee orientation sessions, at company gatherings, and via weekly email messages.

5. When awards are given, do it with a large audience and lots of fanfare and excitement.

6. Track your acquisition (cost per hire) costs, historically and for the referral program. Ensure that management understands the costs of comparable options, whether it is a much larger internal recruiting staff or fees paid to outside sources (headhunters, etc.).

7. Do not rely on your referring employee to manage more than a favorable introduction and a firm endorsement of your company as a great employer. The interviews, reference checks, and corporate sales job are best done by the people who do it full time. Incorporate the referring person in the sales process whenever possible, but manage the process independently.

8. Obtain a firm commitment from senior management for the duration of the referral program. Usually the momentum is very modest until three or four are hired and their sponsor rewarded.

9. Set specific standards for referral submissions, not to disqualify any legitimate leads, but to ensure that there are no conflicts among employees regarding who made the referral first and deserves the award.

10. Consider a modest anniversary award to the referring employee. It can serve to remind and reinforce the motivation to sell the company to colleagues outside.

11. Incorporate referrals into the travel objectives for trade shows, professional conventions, and other company sponsored trips where new contacts are made or renewed.

12. Publish a brief referral manual that not only lays out the qualification rules, but provides tips about finding good job candidates and jogging the memory—i.e., college yearbooks, professional journals, alumni reports.

Just how effective are employee referral programs? For many leading organizations such as Microsoft or Cisco Systems, employee referrals represent 30-40% of new hires. When you consider that the average professional cost-per-hire can cost in the neighborhood of $7,000 - $12,000, employee referrals represent a significant cost saving over traditional recruitment methods. More importantly, however, you will have a new employee who has been briefed on your benefits programs, who understands the company culture, and who has been recommended by a company member. That is not a bad recipe for a successful career.

## Advertising

Employment advertising represents the traditional, tried and true method at attracting talent to your organization. The concept is simple: your organization writes an ad where you describe the job along with the requirements necessary for satisfactory performance. You then place the advertisement in a media outlet that gets it in front of potential employees. The hope is that a few good employment prospects are enticed to mail, fax, or email you a copy of their resume. Response rates to advertisement can range from zero resumes generated to a potential windfall that would put Santa Claus to shame!

The success of any advertising method varies with the type of media you use, the type and size of the audience you reach, the location of the ad, and lastly, the content and style of the ad. In the sections below we discuss the types of media employers are currently using for placing employment ads. When evaluating each method for your use please keep in mind the type of employee / skill set you are trying to attract. Each media source has both strengths and weaknesses as it relates to the type and size of audience it reaches. Consider the needs for finding an administrative assistant vs. an investment banker. Odds are, the local newspaper would serve as an adequate source to advertise for an administrative assistant. But what about an investment banker? Those folks are found in New York, making either the *New York Times* or bankingjobs.com a better selection. Another point to keep in mind is to always determine the size and demographics of each media source. Every resource should make that data available to you, the advertiser. You want to know what kinds of eyeballs you are renting.

Another key question to ask is: "Will the person that my company needs to hire actually see this advertisement?" They might not be looking for a job at all; they may read other periodicals or online advertisements.

Whatever you do, measure your success by the number of high quality resumes and applications obtained, not a simple count of the total resumes received. One evaluation technique is to place a high dollar value on the good resumes and assign a modest negative processing cost to the clearly unqualified. For example, if you assign a $500 value to the good resumes and a negative $5.00 to the useless ones, you can objectively evaluate the success of different job advertisement venues.

Every job advertisement of any kind should include a number that identifies both the position that is open and the media used. This allows multiple ads and a controlled assessment of the productivity of each. You can request that respondents sending resumes include that number for prompt consideration. For example, opening 5392001 can have the designation 5392001-05 for the *New York Times* and 5392001-08 for the *Charlotte Observer*.

Our goal in this section is to cover most of the available advertising methods used by employers. These include the traditional Sunday classifieds plus new Internet strategies. We expect more methods and creative variations of delivering employment advertising will evolve as the need to attract talent becomes more mission critical in the coming decades. Today we are seeing employment ads on billboards and in movie theatres. Tomorrow they may be on coasters, t-shirts, and flashed on the Goodyear Blimp at football games! If you see any novel approaches being used please drop us a line— we would love to hear about it!

## Newspaper

The Sunday classifieds are the definitive traditional method to advertise for employees. It has become almost an American tradition to search through the job ads on Sunday morning at your breakfast table while eating a bagel or grits and drinking coffee. The afternoon and evening can then be spent preparing cover letters and attaching your resume for an early Monday morning drop into the mailbox. A new twist to the Sunday classifieds is the placement by many newspapers of their classifieds on the Internet. An example is CareerPath.com (Figure 3.1). On this Internet site dozens of major newspapers have teamed together to collectively build one of the largest jobs databases on the net.

Advertising in the Sunday classifieds is as easy as calling in an ad to your local newspaper ad office and giving your credit card number by phone. No doubt about it, the Sunday classifieds do work. Anyone who has ever placed a general administrative assistant ad on Sunday in a major daily understands the effect of the ad when they need a wheel barrow to haul away the responses. The plusses of the Sunday paper are the general acceptance of the media and ease of reaching a wide local audience. On the minus side, newspaper ads can be ex-

Figure 3.1: Careerpath.com Web site

tremely expensive and the amount of junk resumes received can be extremely high.

If you need to place ads in multiple markets, we suggest your organization obtain a copy of *Bacon's Newspaper Directory*. It contains a state by state listing of over 27,000 print outlets along with contact and circulation information.

## Top Tips for Effective Newspaper Recruiting

- Write ads that effectively describe the job and the skills necessary for success.

- Include email and corporate Web site addresses.

- Talk to the newspaper account reps to understand what section is effective for your type of ad (professional vs. management vs. technical).

- If your company spends over $100,000 per year on newspaper advertisements, consider using a recruitment advertising agency.

- Consider signing long term contracts if you advertise frequently.

- Make it easy for readers to spot your ads by using a distinctive format and graphics consistently in all of your print ads.

- Incorporate some excitement in the ad; sell your company and the opportunity.

- Treat newspaper ads and Internet ads as two distinct venues; the typical newspaper ad is not effective on the Internet.

## Internet Advertising

The Internet will emerge in the next dozen years as the main vehicle for job advertisements. More importantly, the Internet is an excellent tool for building the talent powered company. The social and technological changes that make the focus on excellence in work performance are a natural complement to the Internet. Some of the general reasons for the fit are:

- The Internet is worldwide in scope. In order to find the job performance stars to staff a talent powered company, recruiters often need candidates that are not found in the local talent pool. With the combination of company job ads, company Web pages, resume databases, and broad research capacities, the Internet has increased the total quantity of persons that can be reached easily by a thousandfold. It has become the savvy recruiter's greatest strategic weapon.

- The costs are incredibly low, as compared to traditional newspaper advertisements. You can run an unlimited number of job ads and search huge resume databases for 24 hours a day during a calendar year for the cost of one Sunday ad in a major newspaper. The savings can even offset a lot of the travel and moving costs associated with hiring someone from across the United States.

- The Internet is an increasingly popular medium, with a high level appeal in the professional, technical, and management ranks, and steadily greater coverage in the general population. It is especially likely that the top performers you need are on the Internet somewhere.

- The Internet has the capacity to tell the whole story about a company, the job, the community, the career opportuni-

ties, the work environment, company benefits, and qualifications required. An innovative manager has a great tool
for pre-selling job candidates on working for a talent powered company.

■ Internet based communications are a good basis for creating and maintaining a comprehensive talent database for
planning current and future growth effectively.

Presently there are 75 million on the Internet worldwide, 40+
million in the United States; and the access costs are dropping to the
point that 80% of the people in the United States can use the job
search resource there, even if only at a school or local public library.
Outside the United States, access is generally limited to the professionals and technical elites who could be eligible for employment in
our talent powered companies. The statistics change overnight on
the Internet, but the large quantities are not as important as the level
of involvement that knowledge workers have in the awesome information resource that is the Internet. The top 20% of the workforce
are on the Internet.

When you compare those costs of the Internet to the per Sunday
ad (one day) costs in the following newspapers, the glaring differen-
tial is obvious. Consider the cost of a 4 x 8 inch display ad in a major
newspaper in the following cities:

■ Atlanta, GA          $5,161

■ Charlotte, NC        $3,622

■ Chicago, IL          $8,640

■ Los Angeles, CA      $9,658

■ New York, NY         $11,104

■ Raleigh, NC          $1,164

And what does it cost to run a similar ad in the most popular Internet job site for 30 days?: $225.

But the impact of the Internet is not limited to the number of users, their desirable performance capacity, or the comparatively low cost of the medium. All those intriguing features are leveraged by the capacity of the Internet to tell the story of your talent powered company to those persons who have the talent to make it successful. The Internet cannot substitute for or outweigh the one-on-one personal communication between an enthusiastic current employee and a future one, but it can open up the lines of idea exchange that make such a direct contact possible.

> ★ The Internet cannot substitute for or outweigh the one-on-one personal communication between an enthusiastic current employee and a future one, but it can open up the lines of idea exchange that make such a direct contact possible. ★

There are currently several thousand job related sites on the Internet which give your organization the ability to advertise your open positions to the masses. While a stable business model for Internet job advertising has yet to be finalized, there exist huge opportunities for organizations to experiment with this new medium. Many of the pioneers in Internet job advertising have discovered and recruited thousands of talented professionals using this resource and have saved their organizations millions of dollars in search firm fees to boot!

There are three main modes for advertising on the Internet. One is the placement of job advertisements in a searchable database such as Hotjobs.com (Figure 3.2) and Monster.com (Figure 3.3). Both are popular job sites who made history by running ads during the 1999 Super Bowl. Another mode of Internet advertising utilized by organizations is to purchase banner advertisements on key Web sites that link to your organization's job information. Figure 3.4 displays four banner ads, which appear on the *Career Magazine* Web site. Jobseekers click on the banners with their mouse and are immediately taken to a recruiting brochure, which attempts to sell them on positions at the advertising organization. Finally, the third mode organizations use to advertise jobs on the Internet is to place them on a corporate Web site. Figure 3.5 displays the recruiting page contained on the Little & Associates corporate Web site.

All three modes of Internet advertising have both plusses and minuses. For additional and more detailed information on Internet job advertising techniques and strategies, see our book *The Employer's Guide to Recruiting on the Internet* by Ray Schreyer and John McCarter

The key distinction between Internet job advertising and more traditional newspaper ads is the increased volume of data one can share with no increase in cost. The typical newspaper ad is a posted notice of an open position; the Internet job ad should be a comprehensive marketing campaign for the job, the work environment, the job location area, and career opportunities at the company.

## Key Internet Job Sites

- www.monster.com
- www.careermag.com
- www.hotjobs.com
- www.careerpath.com
- www.careermosaic.com

# Magazines

Magazines make excellent vehicles for targeted job advertising because hundreds of magazines are available that reach specific population groups and labor markets. Just about every industry group has

Figure 3.2: Hotjobs.com Web site

Figure 3.3: Monster.com Website

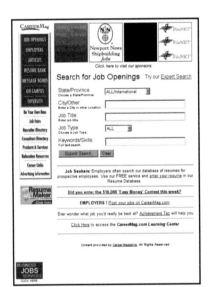

Figure 3.4: Career Magazine Website
with Banner Ads

Figure 3.5: Little & Associates
Recruiting Page

some form of magazine that accepts recruitment job ads. The drawback with magazines is the lead-time required to place an ad (normally 1-2 months). This may not work for organizations who demand "Just In Time" hiring practices. We suggest you consult *Bacon's Guide to Magazines* for information on specific publications that reach your desired audience.

Another suggestion is to consult with employees who are currently doing the same or related jobs. Ask them for the names of associations or professional organizations where they maintain memberships. Consult with the hiring manager on the kinds of periodicals good job candidates should be reading. Include in your options for entry-level jobs, the alumni magazines for institutions that produce many qualified job candidates. Research trade publications as well for your industry and that of key suppliers and customers. Odds are, you will find a magazine or newsletter that will reach your targeted audience.

As an added feature, many magazines and newsletters have Web sites that also accept job advertising. This may be a way to immediately get your jobs in front of readers since the Internet is an immediate medium.

In early 1999, John was working on an assignment to find a vice-president of Human Resources. One of the advertising sources John chose was *HR News,* a monthly HR periodical. He noticed that for a slightly larger fee they would include the advertisement on their Web site. John chose that option and the first day the advertisement hit the Web he received over 100 resumes from well-qualified HR professionals nationwide. The Web based service worked so well that by the time the advertisement hit the periodical John had nearly 1000 resumes in hand from the Web and was well on the way to making a selection.

# Billboards

Yes, organizations more and more are using billboards to attract candidates. On a recent drive down a main thoroughfare in our hometown of Charlotte, NC, we found a billboard advertising for construction workers. We would caution about erecting an employment billboard on the main thoroughfare leading to your competitors corporate offices, but if you do, please send us a picture of it so we can include it in the next edition of this book.

In addition to the immediate responses received, repeated billboard exposure tends to develop a company image and promote name recognition in the communities where billboards are used effectively. If you are experiencing rapid growth or high turnover, billboards can be one source of steady applications.

The appeal of the billboard is the relatively captive audience. The challenge is to create an eye-catching message and incorporate an easy way to contact you. An easy to remember Web site address is often the best choice for many professional jobs. A simple telephone number helps with the others.

# Radio and Television

The tight labor market of the past decade has driven organizations to pull out all the stops in attracting candidates. In recent years we have witnessed a rise in radio and television recruitment advertising. Typically an organization which is new to a city or which has a major need in a specific area runs 30 second spots introducing their organization, discussing their specific needs, and giving additional contact information such as a job hotline or Web site. Advertising for specific jobs is usually not cost effective unless you have a large number of openings for single job titles and the local labor market has large numbers of qualified job candidates. Often the applicants come from competitors.

The advent of cable and the dawning of new technologies such as HDTV will create additional avenues for utilizing television for job advertising. Job channels are already popping up on cable channels and the additional channel content afforded HDTV will provide additional real estate for stations to fill in with appealing content. Maybe your organization can be a pioneer in these new avenues and technologies?

## Movie Theatres

Movie chains are beginning to run advertising prior to the start of a movie. On a recent trip to the cinema we noticed a slide show being run on the main screen. Interspersed among ads for floral, dental, and insurance services was an advertisement for tellers at one of the local banks. Another story we picked up over the newswires was about a graphics development firm who ran ads for graphics designers, developers, etc. at movie theatres before the recent Star Wars episode. Such creative spirit by organizations can only enhance a corporate image to like minded potential employees.

## Internal Communications

One of the sad facts of American business life is that many organizations are blessed with extremely creative, talented individuals, who are either misplaced, underutilized, or pigeonholed in slots within their organization. Utilize every means possible to communicate to your existing talented staff about your needs. Utilize company bulletin boards, company newsletters, your intranet site, and email. Not only will you

> ★ **Utilize every means possible to communicate to your existing, talented staff about your needs.** ★

get some internal gems to step forward, you will get employees recommending friends and colleagues who meet the requisite job profile.

The stumbling block is often a human resources policy that severely restricts internal transfers. In a tight labor market, the person who concludes that he or she must leave the company to be treated fairly, often will. If you want to retain highly talented staff, they need the freedom to change their responsibilities without conducting a job search campaign.

Internal job advertising should be coordinated with any referral compensation and recognition program. Whenever possible, begin your search campaign internally and early, then expand it to the outside if the results are inadequate.

## Creating a Web of Influence

In the last several years a strategy for advertising has emerged that leverages all key advertising components into an integrated holistic approach to attracting talent to your organization. We call this strategy, "Creating a Web of Influence." Key components include:

- An Internet based professionally designed corporate recruiting brochure. The brochure must fully describe the organization: the culture, company history, benefit programs, work locations, and all available job openings. The brochure's focus must be to sell candidates on why they would want to transfer their career to this organization. Include some form of application or resume submittal process so candidates can easily apply for a position.

- A major banner or hyperlink from your main company homepage to the corporate recruiting brochure.

- Job ads placed in appropriate databases on the Internet which describe individual jobs in detail but which also have hyperlinks to the corporate recruiting brochure.

- Banner ads placed on appropriate venues, which link to the corporate recruiting brochures.

- Listing the company name and Web address with all relevant industry specific directories, both Web based and in print.

- Inclusion of company recruiting brochure Web address in all types of recruitment advertising whether in the newspaper, radio, magazines, etc.

- Inclusion of company homepage address on all employee business cards and company correspondence.

Once all elements of this strategy are in place your organization will immediately begin to see job candidates appear from the most unlikely of sources. Here are some of the pathways that candidates used to find jobs at one architectural firm in Charlotte, NC:

- An architect passes her business card out to several colleagues at an American Institute of Architects meeting. The business card contains the company Web address, which in turn links to the company recruiting brochure and current job openings. Over the next year several resumes are generated as architects at competing firms access the Web site and monitor the available openings.

- A student graduates from a leading design school in California and decides he wants to move to North Carolina. He does an Internet search for North Carolina architecture firms in Yahoo. He sees a listing for our firm in Charlotte, NC, clicks to access information on the homepage, and then accesses the recruiting brochure and job listings. A resume is sent within minutes.

■ An ad for an architect for the firms DC office appears in the *Washington Post.* It contains the company homepage address. A senior architect views the ad and does some research on the organization via the Net. After seeing the additional opportunities in Charlotte he decides to consider a move to North Carolina. A resume is sent within minutes.

The only challenge with the "Creating a Web of Influence" strategy will be in attempting to keep statistics on sources of resumes. By linking all advertising sources together it will become hard to determine what ad or event caused the candidate to actually send in their resume. At this point you will need to use your best judgement as to what pieces of the strategy work the best.

## Managing a Network of Talent

One of the technological changes that rivals the Internet in potential impact on the recruiting process is computer data base storage. With well developed, easy to use databases and incredibly cheap storage—hard disks, CD-ROM, tape drives, and optical devices, most companies can retain any job candidate data they manage to collect. Even more important, companies can keep the data available for sophisticated sorts, searches, and communications. At this point in time, it is economically feasible for most companies to save electronically the resumes and job applications for every good job candidate they contact

Additionally, if they invest in communications software and correctly store the Internet address of job candidates, companies can request updated resumes every two years and tell those job candidates about recent advances in corporate career opportunities and general growth. This strategy will enable companies to quickly and directly contact likely candidates for open positions. The job advertising process will function primarily to constantly update the database of critical job skills outside the company.

## Active Methods

The full-employment market of the late 90's has created a major shift in the use of active methods to find talent. Traditional advertising is passive in nature, whereby candidates have jobs or opportunities dangled in front of them and they themselves only have to respond by either sending in a resume or contacting someone in corporate staffing. Active methods are much more cavalier in their approach. They include actively researching and targeting key individuals in the community, at competitors, and directly approaching them about the opportunities within your workplace.

> ★
>
> Active methods include actively researching and targeting key individuals in the community, at competitors, and directly approaching them about the opportunities within your workplace.
>
> ★

## Headhunting

The most traditional approach to actively seek out talent is to hire an executive search consultant. Known as headhunters, these individuals are hired mercenaries who actively seek out and call potential candidates about the available opportunities within your firm. In general there are two types of search consultants: contingency or retained.

A contingency recruiter gets paid if and when he makes the placement. This winner-take-all approach attracts a lot of recruiter energy to the jobs that are perceived as being easy to fill quickly, and employers usually place job orders with more than one search consultant to get the best results for their investment. In contrast, a retained search firm is hired to conduct the search and is paid up front for their efforts, usually partial payments on a fixed progress schedule. Typically a retained search firm has established a long-standing, close relationship with their client and is hired to conduct job searches exclusively.

Both kinds, contingency and retained search, rely heavily on personal knowledge of the special skills their client needs in a job candidate and on a comprehensive database of eligible persons. The database is especially vital for successful contingency recruiters because they are in a hectic race with each other. The job ad is used mostly for extremely hard to fill jobs and to update the database with more candidates.

Both types of recruiting efforts can be rather expensive with recruiter fees amounting to 25-35% of the candidate's first year salary. Add to it the travel, lodging, and meal expenses for conducting interviews with candidates along with relocation costs, and the typical expense to bring an individual on board can account for 50-75% of their first year's salary.

If you desire to use an executive search firm, we suggest you consult the annual *Directory of Executive Recruiters* published by Kennedy Publications. It has over 1,300 pages of information about specialized search consultants. It is available at your local bookstore or through Impact Publications (www.impactpublications.com).

## Research Firms

A hybrid of the active approach is developing in the marketplace whereby for a specific fee, generally $3,000 - $5,000, a firm can be hired to source and pre-qualify several dozen candidates for a particular position. One firm that has heavily marketed their services is known as CORS (www.cors.com). They offer several types of products, which provide client companies with various levels of candidate information. In one package, they provide a detailed report about information on 30 professionals who meet your company's job description and who are within your targeted industry and geography. They also report such background data as experience, qualifications, home address, and salary, plus interest in a career opportunity.

With the advent of the Internet, we anticipate employee research to become a more potent force in employment services offered to corporate HR departments. Such a service offers a cost conscious organization the ability to source available talent at a greatly reduced fee. The challenge with using this type of service remains with the contact portion of the recruiting process. Unlike advertising, where a candidate expresses interest, employee research yields a list of potential candidates, who have not expressed interest in your organization and who have not requested a call. The tricky part is determining what stance your organization takes regarding raiding competitors' employees? Or a better question is—how would you feel if your major competitor began aggressively calling and wooing your valued staff?

## Resume Banks

Currently there are millions of resumes contained on the Internet in various resume banks. Most job boards such as Hotjobs.com and Monster.com have a resume bank component that enables job seekers to store resumes online that can be used to apply for specific employment opportunities on the board. The jobseeker sees a job she might be interested in, then clicks the appropriate button to route her resume to the potential employer automatically on the Internet.

Other technology allows job candidates to file an anonymous resume with a masked return email address. The company expresses interest by emailing back the "anonymous candidate" and the candidate then decides whether to move forward and send forth his or her actual contact information. This is especially advantageous for job candidates that do not want their current employer to discover that they are looking around for more promising career opportunities.

As an added feature, the job boards sell to employers the right to access the resume database and thereby peruse all the available resumes. Several of the boards have resume databases numbering over 100,000. A few have actually reached the million mark!

The question is, are there any good resumes in resume banks? The answer is definitely yes, but recruiters often spend a significant amount of time weeding through volumes of junk resumes to find that jewel of a candidate. The folks that utilize resume banks the most are executive search and staffing organizations. With the potential of a five-figure fee for a placement they are all over the resume banks on an hourly basis. It only takes one placement a month for these folks to assure themselves a new Mercedes in the driveway and a membership to the local country club.

Another resume bank you should consider tapping into is your own corporate resume database. You do have one, right? With the advent of intranets, every organization should have an online database of current employees that additionally lists all their knowledge, skills, abilities, and competencies. That software programmer with a specialty in Easytrieve just may be one floor above you working on another software system today, but may be able to solve your current programming nightmare before he heads home for dinner. A searchable database of internal talent just might be what your organization needs!

## Direct Mail Marketing

Direct mail marketing is a novel approach whereby your organization purchases lists of individuals who have a certain occupation or specialty. Such an approach can be very expensive when you consider the cost of purchasing a list of potential names (can cost 5-10 cents per name), the cost of postage (33 cents via first class mail), plus the development of a marketing brochure. If you are able to purchase a highly targeted list and the job in question is exceedingly hard to fill then by all means direct mail marketing may be your ticket to success.

Another "spin" on the direct mail marketing approach is to purchase email lists of individuals and send out thousands of email messages to potential candidates. Lists are available for purchase over the Internet for various regions of the country, by specific income levels, and by specific occupation. Such approaches are inexpensive and can produce results but come with baggage. This approach is also considered "spam" and represents bad Internet manners. While you may find candidates you might also tarnish your organization's reputation.

## Buy a Competitor

This approach is fast becoming an accepted means of adding to staff. When an organization is in dire need of talent, when the newspaper and Internet ads produce little results, and when your largest customer calls and demands action, why not take the easy way out— buy your competition. This approach will definitely have both plusses and minuses and we do recommend your organization conduct the appropriate Due Diligence exercises to ensure sound business justification of the purchase.

## The Final Challenge—Internal Recruiter Motivation

The biggest hurdle organizations now have to face regarding finding talent is with the talent needed to find the talent. The recruiting profession is hotter than ever. Professionals who are adept at finding, attracting, and hiring talented individuals can be an organization's most strategic asset.

> ★ A successful recruiter totally understands the needs of the business and is adept at identifying pools of candidates and making successful marriages between outside candidates and inside job openings. ★

But unfortunately, many organizations do not understand their value. Recruiting is the talent acquisition arm of the organization. The recruiter's job is part marketing, part counseling, and a major part sales. A successful recruiter totally understands the needs of the business and is adept at identifying pools of candidates and making successful marriages between outside candidates and inside job openings.

However, most organizations place recruiting in the HR department—a place traditionally bound by a myriad of rules, little innovation, and low compensation. The best recruiters often do one of two things: leave recruiting for a position elsewhere in HR (less stress), or leave the organization and enter an executive staffing firm (excellent pay for performance).

Many human resource departments have created their own "Catch 22" paradox with regard to recruiter qualifications and compensation. It works this way:

- We don't pay recruiters very much, give promotions, or give them broad human resource responsibilities such as

Finding Talent

exit interview, retention interviews, or salary administration because they are relatively new, inexperienced, and wouldn't be a recruiter if they were serious about a human resource career in our company.

- We pay outside recruiters (headhunters) handsome fees to recruit senior management, professionals, and specialized technical persons for our company because our recruiters are relatively new and inexperienced. We prefer to work with dedicated professionals who understand the type of people we really need.

- When one of our recruiters does show extraordinary talent and recruiting productivity, we are constrained by pay equity and salary administration policy from paying him or her significantly more than the much less effective colleagues on our recruiting staff.

- We also withhold management and HR training, senior management contacts, and broadening human resource experience (like exit interviews, retention contacts, and salary administration) because we don't intend to promote the marginal producers and the stars don't stay long anyway.

- We often employ the stars as headhunters after they leave because of their in-depth understanding of the type of people we need. (They discovered those insights on the sly.)

- All our competitors and other human resource professional colleagues use the same approaches.

The challenge for your organization is to begin harnessing the talent of your talent acquisition team. Treat them well, compensate them fairly, and accept them as true business partners who have an integral part in your organization's success.

# 5

## ATTRACTING TALENT

The ability to attract talent—to actually move individuals to seek out more information about your organization, to express an interest in your firm, and to have the desire to become part of your team—is another piece of the recruiting process that talent powered organizations have mastered. Like a magnet, these organizations have the knack of obtaining resumes from the top graduating students in the nation, they have workers line up at their offices to fill out applications for employment, and they are universally loathed by headhunters as a place where employees rarely leave and placement fees are never generated. There are three levels of attraction that these organizations generally have engineered which consistently gets their recruiting efforts in high gear.

The first is a generalized attraction that individuals have to them because of their reputation, industry standing, or general good will. The second level of attraction involves individuals being drawn to them based on the pay, benefits, and environment they offer to their employees. Finally, the third level of attraction is the attraction created by their recruiting staff and interviewers during the initial screening calls and interview process. In this stage they practice the art of hospitality, goodwill, and caring which speaks to the hearts of their candidates. By mastering all three levels, these companies are able to hire the best and leave the competition envious of their staffing successes.

Your organization's challenge, if you desire to mirror their successes and join the ranks of talent powered companies, is to begin implementing changes to enhance the perception of your firm in the eyes of outside candidates. They must hold you in high regard, believe you treat your staff exceedingly well, and see you as the employer of choice. It is an enviable goal, requires discipline and imagination to achieve, and cannot be reached overnight. Most of the difficulty in becoming a talent powered company lies in entrenched attitudes and policies that have some business value, but are mostly out of step in the current market for top quality people.

## Level One—Creating a Sphere of Influence

NASA never had a problem after their objectives became part of a national vision. As their reputation grew in the 60's with successive inspiring space shots they became the dream employer of every budding engineer, scientist, and aviation candidate. Is there an animator who has not thought of a career with Disney, or a medical student who could not see him or herself making rounds at the Mayo Clinic? These are just a small example of organizations that have built their reputation as being the best at what they do. On a less visible level, many industries have leading organizations that are the best at what they do. They are the innovators, their reputation is well known within their chosen industry and profession. They are the model organizations that college students wish to have on their resume as an intern experience. They have the best clients; they have the most talented staff. Most importantly, their alumni are leaders in the profession, and they always attract and retain the highest caliber of talent— with an ease rarely matched in their industry.

The first step to becoming a talent powered organization is to raise the stature of your enterprise in the eyes of your industry and/ or profession. In the words of *Field of Dreams*, "If you build it, they will come." While it may take decades to achieve the success of a NASA, Disney, or the Mayo Clinic, remember that two entrepreneurs named Ben and Jerry started a small ice cream business which now enjoys a nationwide reputation. Consider also the two inventors named Steve who started a PC business in their garage. It

> ★ The first step to becoming a talent powered organization is to raise the stature of your enterprise in the eyes of your industry and/or profession. ★

may seem a daunting task, but building your reputation to create you own "Sphere of Influence" within your industry will have some immediate and many long term attraction benefits.

## Key Steps to Increasing Your Organization's Sphere of Influence

- Develop a reputation for excellence and enthusiasm in everything you do.

- Create a working environment that emphasizes vision and performance.

- Conduct all business interactions in a highly professional manner.

- Insist that all business cards, marketing brochures, and related office materials are professionally designed, of high quality, and project an image befitting a successful organization.

- Forge relationships with the media. Look for opportunities to have your experts comment on stories related to your industry.

- Have your management get involved in the community via United Way, Habitat for Humanity, Arts Council, Boy Scouts, etc.

- Offer internships and mentoring opportunities for local students.

- Get involved with the Chamber of Commerce. Make sure senior leaders in your organization obtain key leadership slots within key Chamber committees.

- Have members of your firm join the appropriate professional organizations, and actively participate in the operations of those groups.

- Make sure you have a fully functional, highly creative, corporate Web site.

## Level Two—Delivering the Message: We Are a Great Place to Work!

The next level of attraction is to create with each and every potential candidate a warm glow about the way your organization rewards, promotes, and treats its employees. Quality pays more than it costs when there is a dynamic, shared vision of organizational goals and the leadership has a strong commitment to nurture its employees in a way that allows them to focus on those goals. The company refuses to make either/or choice between creating a selfless missionary endeavor or a highly competitive, individual driven political rat race. Instead, talent powered companies elect to foster a leadership culture where routine employee needs are met routinely and persons are rewarded for their achievements. There is more leadership than authority, more challenges than policies, more imagination than controls, and so much success that there are few fights over who gets the credit.

In other chapters we fully discuss strategies for creating a great work environment. Once that work environment has been created your next challenge is to inform all potential job candidates. As an initial venue to get the word out, your employees will do an excellent job of informing their friends about all the benefits of working for your organization. But besides the constant positive comments from happy employees, you need to capture the essence of your environment in several types of media and find ways to deliver the message to potential job candidates.

## Key Steps to Getting the Word Out

- Describe your work environment in all newspaper ads and other forms of recruitment advertising; be clear and decisive about all the positive features of the jobs there—the community, the schools, the benefits, the team work mentality, and supportive management.

- Produce a recruiting brochure, which clearly defines all the positive benefits of working for your organization.

- Have a list of employees available to potential employees to give informational interviews about your organization.

- Produce a video displaying a "day in the life" at working in your organization.

- Construct a recruiting Web site and include links to it from all Internet job advertisements.

- Have an open house for the community.

- Run job ads in local high school papers, college periodicals, and other lost cost venues where job candidates or the people who influence them can see data on your company.

- Follow our advice on Internet job advertising in Chapter 4 and in our book, *The Employer's Guide to Recruiting on the Internet.*

- Issue press releases about product development, quality improvements, and employee generated innovations.

- Create and maintain links to influential mentors at educational institutions that are major sources of outstanding job candidates. Encourage your employees to keep in touch as well. Periodically award cash and a nice plaque to some employee's most inspiring instructor, teacher, or professor.

- Send top-flight representatives to trade shows and professional meetings; encourage them to write technical articles for presentation and publication.

- Develop a corporate alumni association—those persons who left the company for greener pastures and would be welcomed if they developed the taste and insight to return. Send them routine company publications and notices.

## Level Three—Person Centered Recruiting

In the age of the Internet, email, electronic resume management systems, psychological assessments, and behavioral based interviews, organizations can often forget that an actual human being is involved in these systems. Successful talent driven organizations understand how to use the technology and how not to allow the technology to use them. With a general shortage of competent persons impacting corporate growth, the talent powered company invests marketing and sales resources in its recruiting efforts. They see the job candidate as a very vital **customer**, one who directly or indirectly enables them to succeed in the

> ★ Talent powered companies have abandoned the concept of job candidates as humble supplicants to be hassled, measured, and hazed the point that they feel lucky if they get a job offer. Instead, they picture the interview and decision process as the first stage in a mutually beneficial career. ★

marketplace. Their recruiting process is designed and engineered to avoid any confusion between when the job candidate is selling their talents and when the recruiter is selling the company. In other words, the "customer" is qualified early and the selling never ends.

Talent powered companies have abandoned the concept of job candidates as humble supplicants to be hassled, measured, and hazed to the point that they feel lucky if they get a job offer. Instead, they picture the interview and decision process as the first stage in a mutually beneficial career. One of the criteria that they use in their recruiting process review is simply, "If the job candidate and the company fail to begin a career relationship immediately following our recruiting effort, will he or she have an impression of our organization that lays the groundwork for a future association?" By recognizing the limited dimensions of the talent pool, and the potential of future relationships, the correct perspective is established.

## Key Attributes of Person-Centered Recruiting

- Recruiters and interviewers treat all candidates as if they are valued customers.

- Focus on the holistic needs of the candidate, not just the job needs—where they will live, what social and recreation needs they have.

- Spend time with candidates—talk about their needs, take them on a community tour, do dinner at a local restaurant, show them the same courtesy and respect as you would to any valued client.

- Be honest with the candidate. Let them hear about the myriad of opportunities within your organization, but also make them aware of potential pitfall and roadblocks.

- Make it clear that they will have a mentor with responsibilities to them and the company for their career progress.

- Celebrate the company's turnover record in the context of a total career employment and a serious commitment to their continued development. If you already have a great turnover record, advertise the fact.

- Be specific and generous about their work environment—office space, team involvement, leadership expectations, work rules, allowances for special clothes, software, replacement of aging furniture, handling of benefit claims, and the total benefit package.

- Ensure that their spouse's concerns and comforts are addressed clearly and quickly. Provide some assistance in house hunting, school locations, and job searches.

- Form a newcomers' group of recent arrivals [the past two years] and encourage an informal meeting with the group for job candidates.

- Arrange a brief lunch with a senior executive whenever possible; pick one of the most personable and company enthusiastic executives and brief her or him on some key features of their talents. Make this a sales opportunity, not another kind of interview.

- Pick a local meeting or event for a job candidate to attend; one that is related to the job candidate's stated interests and/or avocations.

- Define the various career paths within the company.

- Advise the candidate of projected assignments during the first month on the job, training options, team memberships, office or other workspace reserved, and also orientation programs.

In short, while completing a due diligence ability and attitude inquiry, ensure that the job candidate realizes that she or he has found a career home.

# 6

# RETAINING EMPLOYEES

The labor markets of the last half-decade have raised the issue of employee retention to the forefront of management issues and imperatives. Consider the myriad of reasons for retention initiatives:

- Replacement costs for employees are running in the neighborhood of 50% or more of a job candidate's first year salary. With turnover rates increasing for critical technical specialists and simply competent other personnel, the replacement costs represent a major increase in compensation expenses without a corresponding increase in productivity. By dividing the average replacement cost percentage by the current average turnover period, we can determine the replacement premium and the general cost of ineffective retention. For example, if a position costs 50% of the first year salary to fill the job and on average, this happens every two years, then the company has a labor cost premium of 25% for the job.

- The downtime and lost productivity caused by a staffing change adds to operating costs and results in significant lost opportunities (with real opportunity costs). In an optimum situation, the new hire has the skills and experience to step in immediately and assume the responsibilities of the job without delay or reduced effectiveness. But more often than not, there is a significant learning curve even for well-qualified candidates. The return to normal levels of excellence and productivity is further complicated by the accumulation of tasks left uncompleted or poorly managed since the departure of the predecessor.

- Talent shortages have strained further the ability of employers to fill empty positions in a timely manner. In many cases, the total number of jobs, open and filled, exceed the number of persons with the minimum qualifications to perform the work. Deficient educational systems and restrictions to developing expertise on-the-job have created awesome gaps in labor supply. Both public neglect of educational institutions and corporate reluctance to make long term investments in a mobile resource have contributed to the situation.

- Departures break up effective teams, wasting development time and unit morale. While teams are an important component of effective retention, when the overall efforts fail, those remaining team members are left to carry on the work. To the extent that the team was either highly interdependent and resource lean, there is a corresponding impact on their output. Added to the learning curve mentioned above, the new person must interact and develop functional relationships with the new teammates.

Many employers have learned that it is far easier to keep their current workforce content and motivated instead of periodically replacing key players. A cottage industry has sprung up with books, seminars, and consultants with a host of quick fix solutions. Some of them even encourage employers to make counter offers to employees who have already emotionally departed, to bribe the person into staying until they find a replacement.

Whether it is a big bonus, day care benefits, a sabbatical, or a combination of other benefits, new approaches are being engineered daily by employers to retain employees and keep them with the company on a long term basis.

Before we begin to discuss the variety of steps that can be taken to retain employees, it is best that we first consider the factors that actually motivate employees and keep them satisfied in their job. Based on several models of motivation, the following conclusions can be drawn from the current research:

> ★
> **Whether it is a big bonus, day care benefits, a sabbatical, or a combination of other benefits, new approaches are being engineered daily by employers to retain employees and keep them with the company on a long term basis.**
> ★

- Individuals are committed to undertaking a job or project when they see a high probability of a valued reward or rewards as outcomes. Rewards may be extrinsic to themselves (money, benefits, promotion, job security) or intrinsic (warm feeling inside, challenge of the work, people they work with, a sense of achievement).

- When individuals undertake a job or project, their performance is based in part on their knowledge, skills and abilities as one factor and their understanding of their role as the second factor. In essence, their abilities drive the quality and quantity of their work, but the understanding of their role and place in the project focuses their efforts down the correct path.

- After individuals perform a job or project, they gain both intrinsic and extrinsic rewards. They immediately compare these rewards to what they perceive as fair and reasonable and ask the internal question, "Am I being treated fairly?" If the answer is yes, then we have satisfaction and increased output and performance. If the answer is no, we have dissatisfaction, decreased output and performance, and furtive job searching. In many cases, the timing of the reward is as important as the financial cost to the organization.

- To the extent that the employer is perceived as arbitrarily delaying rewards, the retention value of those rewards is devalued and discounted. Indefinite delays and circumstances beyond the control of employees can become a major disincentive if management is perceived as weaseling out of their commitments to the persons providing tangible results. This is especially damaging if recognition and other less tangible rewards are withheld to avoid contemplation of the broken promises.

- During tenure with their company, people's loyalties are influenced greatly by the quality of support provided during the crises of their lives. When a parent dies, when a child is seriously ill, when a car is totaled in an accident, or a fire destroys part of a home, the company that is opened minded about its employees' stress and flexible about work expectations will reinforce current ties and develop new ones.

- To some extent, based on individual personality and general socialization, the value of a work experience and the various compensations received depends on both the individual's evaluation of the rewards received and the opinions of colleagues, friends, and family about the compensation. For the person who performs well in teamwork situations and values that environment highly, it is very likely that she or he will also share the perceptions and biases of those they like and respect.

- Participation in a self-managed, successful work team is in itself a strong motivator. Often loyalty to a work team offsets the distress that its members experience through affiliation with the company. There is an offsetting negative effect if differences with management are widely felt and frequently shared.

## Point One

Some factors need to be kept at the forefront in considering this research. Rewards can be anything that a person values: it may be a title, an attractive office, a nurturing work team, a good chair, a window, bonuses, a thank you, a seminar, travel, a talented boss, four weeks vacation, daycare, flextime, or challenging assignments.

In addition, rewards that individuals value vary with time and the stage of their career and life. New college grads desire the opportunity to learn and grow, test their mettle, and prove their competence. Retirement benefits have little reward impact to them at this point because they have a limited interest in the remote future.

Then there are the 40+ year old business professionals. They have gone to college, obtained their bachelors and possibly advanced degrees and have worked in industry for 20+ years. They have proved themselves in their chosen profession and now look forward at retirement creeping up in 20 years or less. Questions of 401k plans, bonuses, retirement benefits, and healthcare will probably be near the top of their reward and concern lists.

Before we can understand what exactly should be done to keep employees, we must understand what each employee values. This is a very daunting task. Everyone varies in his or her likes and dislikes. Our challenge is that we often over generalize about what the average person believes and thus drive off quality individuals who have different reward values from the norm. In a nutshell, the more you can tailor rewards to each specific individual, the better you can retain.

*Sally is considering a position with both Big Company and Little Company USA. They have made her similar offers except that Little Company USA offers a flexible healthcare program whereby if you do not choose the company health benefits, the funds normally spent on your healthcare by the organization are distributed to you in your paycheck. Big Company offers employees healthcare whether they need it or not. Since Sally is already covered under her spouse's healthcare plan she will see an addition $2,000 salary increase from Little Company's flexible plan.*

## Point Two

The concept of equity has a major impact on an individual's satisfaction and desire to stay in a certain job or project. If individuals believe that they are not receiving a fair reward for the effort they are giving with their input, they will often become dissatisfied, disillusioned, and leave. Any facts about comparative salaries in the industry or the immediate area become irrelevant in the face of that perception. Often a transition in thinking is necessary.

If you were to lose one of your top performers, what kind of salary and benefits would you be willing to offer to get someone with the same skills and experience? The optimum point between a person's current salary and the company's desperation price is often closer to the former than to the latter, but if the gap is too wide for too long, an employee is very likely to leave and stay gone.

Your organization must spend a considerable amount of effort to ensure that pay and reward systems are delivered on a fair and equitable basis, and are recognized as such. Also, please consider that everything has the potential of being seen as a reward: the size of office, time spent with the boss, types of projects, etc. If you understand what everyone in your workgroup values, you will better be able to match rewards with specific individuals and understand when you have a balanced and equitable situation. As mentioned above, the timing of rewards can have a dramatic impact on their effectiveness for retention. Waiting for earned rewards places an undue strain on employee loyalty.

We began by discussing the individual and motivation. In a perfect world we would be able to treat each and every person on an individual basis: design a work environment and reward system that meets their particular needs at this exact point in their career and life. Unfortunately, such a world does not exist. Rather it is important to keep the individuals needs in mind while implementing system wide reward programs that are effective.

## Major Determinants of Employee Retention

### Challenging Work

Research has conclusively found that when individuals successfully accomplish mentally challenging work, they are more satisfied and happy. People thrive on being given the opportunity to "rise to the occasion" and "test their mettle." They desire exciting, challenging work that gives them the ability to exercise and expand their skills, and forces them to learn and adapt to new situations. To retain the best it is imperative that your organization consistently ensures that your employees, especially the ones you have identified as top talents, are feeling challenged in their work situation.

▶ Specific Strategies

■ Meet with all employees to determine what pieces of their job "light their fire."

- Understand each staff members limits and abilities.

- Challenge them to new levels of performance with important, demanding, and challenging assignments.

- Ensure that adequate training and education is provided to employees so that they have a reasonable expectation of achieving their challenging goals.

- Guard against "pigeonholing" talent due to high demand needs. Top talent becomes very uncomfortable on the shelf.

- Keep on the lookout for repetitive, dull employment situations that may create burnout in your workforce. Look for opportunities to organize tasks and utilize software to avoid having $50/hour talent performing $8/hour tasks.

## Personally Interesting Work

Everyone has likes and dislikes, areas of passion and excitement. Individuals will stay and be more satisfied in an organization where they are able to work on jobs or projects that they find personally interesting. The architect who has a passion for the outdoors and is a member of the Sierra Club may jump at the chance of designing a new office park which is to be built according to "environmentally friendly standards."

### ▶ Specific Strategies

- Get to know your staff and their passions.

- Do your best to integrate their passions into their work.

- Help them transfer to another department or position, if necessary to help them find work that is exciting for them. Sharing talent with other units is a better solution than losing staff to other companies. It also increases the probability that the person will choose to return to your unit in the future.

- Continually monitor the types and levels of the work of your staff. Make sure some of each employee's day contains some passionate work!

## Just Compensation and Pay

People demand to be compensated fairly and equitably with others in their job, profession, and industry. In addition, they desire to be kept abreast of how the organization is growing financially and to be rewarded for their contribution to its success. The # 1 reason cited by over 60% of individuals in a recent study as to reasons to accept or leave a job was compensation. Pay and compensation do matter, especially now

> ★
> **The #1 reason cited by over 60% of individuals in a recent study as to reasons to accept or leave a job was compensation.**

that retirement programs and long term employment contracts between worker and company are less common, though highly desirable.

### ▶ Specific Strategies

- Research pay and compensation levels for positions in your organization.
- Adjust levels as needed to create balance and equity.
- Institute a performance based bonus system.
- Establish a policy of long term employment; only discharging those who cannot or will not perform at expected levels.
- Have available spot bonus and rewards for performers who do outstanding efforts.

- Consider stock options and other financial incentives.

- Surprise employees with timely compensation improvements.

## Satisfactory Working Conditions

Employees want to work in a clean, comfortable surrounding. Whether it is an office job in a high rise or an auto repair shop, employees are much more happy and satisfied if their surroundings are neat, orderly, and clean. A recent study conducted by the American Society of Interior Designers found that the most important attributes people want in a physical workspace are (in order of importance): cleanliness, visual appeal, well-lit and bright, new furniture and equipment, access to people and equipment, quiet and privacy, comfortable furniture, good air quality, nice windows, and a view.

### ▶ Specific Strategies

- Have a replacement plan for used and old furniture.

- Spend lavishly on improving worker meeting facilities, break and locker rooms, and office furniture.

- Buy the "good stuff" such as in Hayworth, Steelcase, and Herman Miller.

- Be sensitive to cube vs. office environments: boomers prefer offices, generation Xers prefer the open environments. But no one appreciates being nickeled and dimed into a personally uncomfortable or counterproductive work environment. The workspace should reflect the work assignments and prevailing corporate vision.

- Ask staff for input on workspace design and layout.

## Trusted and Respected Managers and Co-workers

The best employees desire and demand to work with other employees and managers whom they can trust and respect. Without trust and respect, no long-term relationships can be built. With the movement in recent years towards team formation, trust and respect are more critical than ever.

### ▶ Specific Strategies

- Obtain employee feedback when doing promotions. Promote only those employees who have earned the respect of their peers and have proven their abilities to communicate, listen, and lead.

- Be cognizant of trust and respect issues when forming work teams of any kind. If the work is consistently team oriented, the people who prefer to be left alone can make only modest contributions and will require special handling.

- Hire individuals who have a track record of integrity and excellent business sense.

## Organizational Policies and Procedures that Support Employee Reward Attainment

Believe it or not, there are many organizations that have established a web of personnel policies and procedures that in effect stop employees from achieving the success they desire. In some cases, elaborate wage and salary policies are created which prevent managers from adequately rewarding employees for superior performance and service. In other cases, corporate rules are created which give needed equipment and resources to workers based solely on such criteria as seniority, title, or position instead of on the basis of actual need. How successful can one be if they cannot get the tools and staff necessary to do the job?

## How Crazy Can it Get?

- In one financial organization there was a rule that the maximum raise or increase per year was capped at 9%. Dozens of employees who had been hired at a below market rate or who had done outstanding work and were unable to benefit financially had to quit their job and then be rehired back at a current market salary.

- In one giant technology organization bonuses were capped at $10,000 for mid-level managers. One acquaintance of ours took over a floundering software department and grew its revenue from $6 million per year to over $150 million. He quit when he received his maximum $10,000 bonus.

- In another financial organization rules were in place whereby the new computer equipment was first given to senior management. The newer employees, who were generally techno-friendly and could do programming in their sleep, were left stranded outside the information highway with old equipment, whereas their boomer bosses were still trying to figure out email on their brand new Pentium class machines. Needless to say the productivity and success of the newer employees suffered due to technology rules based on positional power instead of positional need!

▶ **Specific Strategies**

- Review all reward policies within the organization.

- Make sure all policies are balanced between protecting the assets of the organization while still being able to offer rewards for performance.

- Step out of the box and put in place reward systems that truly let your top performers know they did an excellent job.

- Survey employees to determine if everyone feels they have access to the appropriate resources necessary for them to succeed.

- Institute career-planning sessions for employees and seek to understand their goals and desires and counsel them on a path for goal and reward attainment.

## Organizational Role Issues

Employees want to know what are their areas of accountability and responsibility. They need to have support in doing their assignments, to receive the appropriate resources, and given an appropriate amount of time to complete the job. Two factors that produce stress in individuals, that in turn leads to job dissatisfaction and turnover, are role-conflict and role-ambiguity. Role-conflict involves the employee being placed in a "Catch 22" situation: this can result from having not enough resources to complete assignments, or not having enough time; or being forced to produce results that will please one manager and displease another.

Role-ambiguity involves the employee not being able to fully understand what is actually required for satisfactory performance on the job. Organization role issues have risen to near the top of turnover issues since most organizations have chosen to "strip away the fat" and run "lean and mean." In such an organization, a few folks exiting the organization can create a chain reaction in which remaining employees face role conflict on a continuing and confusing basis.

► **Specific Strategies**

- Talk to employees and managers constantly about their needs and what is required of them, avoiding surprises.

- Be vigilant to fill in performance gaps caused by employee turnover or extended absences. The ability of teams to carry the load is temporary at best, and perpetual overloads cripple morale.

- Institute a practice of outlining each employee's zone of responsibility, and encouraging self-managed work teams to do the same .

## Fringe Benefits

The benefits area is one place where your organization can get highly creative and offer a host of extra perks that will both impress and create a warm feeling in the minds of your employees. Begin with the basics of offering standard benefits such as: healthcare plan; dental; life insurance; employee assistance program. There are two essential questions to ask about any benefits package—does it help employees focus on the job while they are at work, laying to one side a large number of routine concerns that the company can help them manage on a cost effective and caring basis? And, does the benefit contribute in a significant way to their life outside the work environment, assisting employees to lead a balanced life without intrusions into their privacy?

► **Specific Strategies**

- Survey the workforce to determine what benefits would be most beneficial to meet their needs.

- Keep abreast of your competition to determine what types of perks and benefits are being offered in your industry.

- Focus on offering benefits that give employees the choice to choose and select among different options.

## Long Term Employment

Few single strategies are as effective as a policy, tradition, or general commitment to long term employment. Contrary to the popular (and therefore questionable) wisdom that long term employment is a historical relic, companies continue to utilize the approach, however quietly. It is not a policy for the weak of heart or mind; some necessary prerequisites are:

1. A disciplined hiring process that attracts good performers and weeds out second rate abilities and attitudes. Work group members participate in the process and the hiring supervisor takes a leading role; no one just accepts whomever the human resources department sends to them.

2. A disciplined performance review process that eliminates the mistakes early and firmly. The work group and the supervisors do not accept barely good enough performance under any circumstance; both can veto either a hiring decision or a retention decision.

3. A comprehensive training program and a learning culture that supports it. Staffing levels allow aggressive training of useful skills.

4. A management group with the courage and insights to innovate and capture new markets, develop new approaches, and generally adapt their talent powered organization to changes in resources and markets.

5. Human resource policies that encourage personal growth and real accomplishment.

## Your Best Retention Ally

The recruiter is a natural for the functions related to retention.

The successful recruiter knows what incentives work in the talent driven marketplace. She or he is using the same or similar carrots to entice experienced outside people to your organization. A "battlefield" exposure to the fight for excellent employees is the best background for insights into keeping them motivated to persevere and produce within their current organization.

A recruiting manager is the best ally of the line manager who wants to retain the people who make a difference in the success of his division or department. Retention is a key line manager function, but few have the time or energy to operate as effectively as a full-time recruiting professional.

The recruiter will also be armed for providing excellent advice if she or he is a routine and effective participant in the exit interview process. On one hand, the recruiter will gain first hand insights into what the competition is offering to attract good performers. The knowledge will guide his or her own recruiting efforts far beyond any professional research or general surveys. First hand accounts may not be as balanced, but are highly reliable.

On the other hand, the recruiter will be armed to provide key retention advice to all levels of management and obtain feedback on her own retention projects. The questions that need to be answered are:

■ What did the leaving employee find wanting at the job being left behind? Was it income, opportunity for advancement, recognition, better work atmosphere, more freedom, more security, less interference, better supervision?

- Was there a serious disconnect between what the current employer promised and what was delivered?

- Did the employee find herself compensating for defects in management practices, company products, and work procedures?

- Did the company make unreasonable and regular demands on the employee's time and energy?

- What specific features of the new job do you find most appealing?

- What would have to change here in order for you to return at some time in the future?

- Are you aware that we value your contributions to the company and we will be interested in discussing future opportunities here?

An exit interview with the recruiter who brought the employee to the company originally can be extraordinarily effective. There should be a personal relationship based on trust that is central to the discussion. Whether or not the employee links the current major dissatisfaction with the recruiter may play a major role in the exchange, but even some verbal fireworks could provide more insights than a cookie cutter type discussion with some HR person that the departing employee never met before the exit interview.

And if exit interviews by recruiters have value, shouldn't the recruiter have some interim discussion during that person's career with the company? Periodic discussions might provide an early warning of difficulties to come and forestall an expensive premature departure. If the relatively new hire is pleased with his new job, he might be willing to recommend some other stars for employment. The best kind of retention is integrated retention—tying together recruiting, retention, and departures in a way that minimizes costs and maximizes the effectiveness of corporate personnel.

If your recruiters have the freedom and incentive to follow up on the career successes and incremental progress of the persons they recruit, won't those relationships create a special opportunity to get an early warning about real problems before recruits become "career serious" about their current position? Very often, managers are stunned, if not alarmed, when one of their people turns in a resignation letter (or two-week notice). The dedicated professional recruiter who regularly contacts the stars she or he discovered can play a pivotal role in anchoring them in your corporate galaxy.

But do companies consider their recruiters to be capable of performing either exit or retention interviews? If they lack the basic skills for those responsibilities, they are certainly underqualifed to perform recruiting functions.

Human resource groups are generally challenged by the variety of roles they are called upon to perform. Too often, apparent or real disinterest in their recruiting functions leads operational managers to bypass them altogether or to only allow them to find entry level hourly staff. As a result, the key recruiting function is outsourced to persons who may be very capable in finding good candidates, but have little motivation or potential to effectively retain.

## The Big Picture

Retention effectiveness grows out of management's appreciation of its importance and their capacity to model and perpetuate the values implicit in the process. Because of its growing prominence as an issue, and its relative obscurity in the immediate past, retention is not an automatic high priority in senior management and the temptation to delegate the responsibilities to some junior manager in human resources is substantial. A training class—modeled after those covering EOCC and diversity issues—may modestly raise awareness, but can hardly make a significant difference.

Retention either becomes a corporate value and policy priority, or the company becomes a docile victim of labor market forces. With the heated pace of technological change, increased competition at home and abroad, and growing regulation of business practices, investments in retention may seem difficult to justify. Effective retention, however, is a part of the solution, not just another problem. Retention is an opportunity to build a large, highly successful team. It is essential to a talent powered company.

# 7

## CREATING A TALENT POWERED COMPANY

T alent powered companies are more than just a collection of competent people. Implicit in their success and continuity is a sense of community that energizes the organization despite occasional business setbacks and the personal problems of individuals. In talent powered companies, an implicit if not explicit interrelationship prevails. There is a broad sharing of ideas, concerns, and aspirations. Because of the atmosphere of trust fostered by management and the commitment to excellence by employees in general, hearty competition takes place without rancor, teams evolve without official sanctions, work is performed without hassling about responsibility, and everyone glows about every success that occurs.

It does sound too good to be true. But most experienced employees have enjoyed a taste of this esprit de corps at least once in their careers, however briefly. It is a natural rush that most people associate with a winning high school sports team, the boiling over of youthful energy, the intoxicating attitude that anything is possible. It can and does happen in organizations of every size and nature.

But essential prerequisites are vision, leadership, and organizational maintenance. Vision is a separate issue despite its frequent link with leadership. Sometimes organizational vision develops with minimal involvement and inspiration from those in authority, evolving from natural leadership of rank and file employees with a passion for success.

Leadership, from whatever source, is essential to sustain momentum and direction through the vicissitudes of extended struggles. The most challenging element, however, is often the routine nurturing of an organization's vitality—the handling of everyday concerns that allows other employees to focus on main objectives with a minimum of distraction.

> ★
> In talent powered companies, an implicit if not explicit interrelationship prevails. There is a broad sharing of ideas, concerns, and aspirations.
> ★

This chapter collects a broad sampling of vision, leadership, and maintenance tasks that people in an organization can perform to stimulate and enable a productive environment. The tasks are not an exhaustive collection, but create a template for investigation and elaboration within the context of a given operation.

## Energy

When you are building a talent powered company, one of the tricky necessities is developing the kind of emotional energy that drives individual initiative and strength of purpose. It is a cheerleader task, with an emphasis on the leader part of that word. The role is accepted gladly by natural and deliberate leaders, but many managers turn their backs on anything representing passion at work. Instead, they restrict enthusiasm of any kind for sports, social events, alumni meetings, hobbies, and significant others. They may have a commitment to their career, but it is a cold, hard determination to have the financial freedom to fund outside interests.

The new adage, "Different strokes for different folks," is only half true regarding the emotional energy needed for a talent-powered company. Successful, competent persons want to feel good about what they do, to receive acclaim for achievement, to taste the thrill of winning, to savor the satisfaction of prevailing against tough odds. When you strip the dreams out of the business plan, pare the enthusiasm from a team building workshop, and outline the bare, cold features of a production goal, you compromise the potential for success.

Some tactics for resurrecting latent enthusiasm are:

- Utilize leaders with obvious enthusiasm; hire some if you must correct a company wide predilection for cold fish management.

- Resurrect applause as a medium of communication. Use it in meetings small and large, develop rituals for its application, and enlist others to promote the practice.

- Honor enthusiasm in your verbal and written communications. Recognize its integral role in success by acknowledging its presence in team and individual accomplishments.

- Train supervisors and managers in the appropriate ways to demonstrate their feelings. Protect them from the stigma of only showing feeling when they are angry or apprehensive.

- Help managers write short, effective, feeling speeches. Suggest that they use Lincoln's Gettysburg address as a model for "to the point" communications. Even adopt the Toastmaster Club's four step guidelines for effective speeches—stand up, speak out, shut up, sit down.

- Enroll supervisors and managers in a Toastmaster Club.

- Recognize and celebrate the contribution that enthusiastic people make to productivity and innovation. Note the role that emotional energy plays in effective leadership.

■ Celebrate, celebrate, celebrate—nothing builds excitement and energy as well as the opportunity to share socially with your trusted friends and colleagues.

## Paying for Productivity—Energizers

As has been discussed elsewhere in this book, salary and wage compensation are great opportunities for motivation and building company commitment, but are too frequently the most painful source of employee discontent. Few things are as damaging to the corporate retention and recruitment processes than a perception, true or not, that the company will sacrifice all the lofty goals of fairness and employee orientation in order to meet the quarterly profit projections.

Some useful guiding principles and tactics are:

■ Surprise your excellent performers with out-of-sequence raises. It may be less of an administrative burden to dispense general pay increases at one time during the year, but the excellent performers deserve both more and earlier. Add some excitement to their lives by making their increase special and unexpected.

■ Distinguish between recognizing one-time accomplishments and long term growth in value to the company. If an employee develops an idea that produces a half million dollar savings, give him or her a bonus that recognizes the size of the contribution, instead of a modest pay raise that seems insignificant in comparison. A fox's share bonus beats a warm handshake pay raise any time.

■ Pay for results instead of potential. Be cautious of "pay for learning programs" that become a sinecure for persons

unwilling to apply advanced skills in the work place. Co-
ordinate valuable in-house staff development training with
operational planning for harnessing those abilities on a day-
to-day basis; especially if the compensation is a long-term
growth of income.

■ Don't depend on pay as a sole response to rewarding employees. Pay is a necessary, but not sufficient, piece of the
compensation pie. Pay is a primary factor because it is a
way to keep score in a competitive society (talented employees know how to keep score), but it cannot be substi-
tuted solely for the normal modes of recognition and appreciation.

■ Look for techniques to cost-effectively enhance employee
quality of life without increasing their tax consequences.
Most employees recognize the large bite that federal and
state taxes take from every pay increase, and place a high
value on a benefits package that reduces their cash expen-
ditures without increasing their taxes.

■ In tandem with tax free or tax reduced benefits, educate
the employees on the value of their total compensation
package. Smart employees will prize the short and long
term benefits of working for a company that looks out for
their well being. Include any corporate retirement package, social security benefits, and disability insurance. Include in the education process opportunities for spouses
to learn about the package.

■ Consider employee stock option programs (ESOPs) to provide additional benefits and to increase the level of their
involvement with the success of the company.

■ Explore strategic stock options for a much larger group of
employees than the executive suite staff, and educate em-

ployees about incorporating the stock options into their retirement planning.

- Encourage retirement planning with 401k and similar programs. But avoid shell game retirement plans whose economies are based on the few participants who actually receive significant benefits.

- Customize special rewards, large and small, to reflect company recognition of excellent performance and longevity— buy an hour in their honor on a public radio station they like, give tickets to a ball game or other event, present company logo accessories and apparel, assign them front row parking spaces, supply magazine subscriptions to work related periodicals, and sponsor an occasional personal 'thank you' from a senior executive.

- Support family-care programs. There is a variety of child care options, both in house and community and commercial based, and many companies turn good child care programs into a strong competitive advantage for retaining critical staff. Adult day care, where available, gives families the option of keeping aging parents at home rather than giving up one job in a two career family or sending their senior citizens to an expensive retirement home away from family and friends.

- Explore charter school opportunities. If local educational opportunities are a critical issue in keeping high quality professionals, a charter school for employees can be a dramatic benefit for recruiting and retaining personnel. This approach can be especially fruitful in remote sites where the educational infrastructure is incomplete. Parents will make career decisions based on their children's needs.

■ Assemble a package of hospitalization, major medical, vision care, dental, and disability insurance that makes a difference in the life confidence level of your employees. Analyze the paperwork burden of each component to ensure that participants are not required to jump through hoops to obtain the normal benefits.

■ Have the information technology department create a company based ISP that provides free or low cost Internet access for employees; supplement that benefit with training for them and their children, and with assistance in acquiring home computers at a discount.

■ Explore personal days off and allow the trade in of sick days for personal days or end of the year cash payments. You can also simply replace sick days with personal days.

■ Develop a list of civic organizations, charities, and colleges for which the company will match contributions up to a certain level, underwriting the generosity of employees.

■ Where both output and quality can be easily measured, establish an incentive plan to reward exceptional performance. Develop the plan so that the growth of productivity will have continued benefits; the payoffs for the company should still be there if output doubles or triples.

■ Discuss compensation with individual employees on a regular basis to assess how well your collection of compensation strategies is effective in building the kind of loyalty you want in good and outstanding performers. Talk to the marginal soreheads as well, but discount their perennial discontent unless their complaints are reflected among the obvious targets for your retention and recruitment efforts.

## Knowledge Worker Environment

Peter Drucker is still on target with his "knowledge worker" concept. The disconnect comes from the easy assumption that the knowledge worker is an evolutionary and inevitable process that requires no activity, personal or corporate, to be achieved. In contrast, our service economy is increasingly dependent on what individuals know and their freedom to take initiatives. The companies that recognize how personal competencies impact their revenue per employee are aggressively promoting skill development in a broad variety of approaches. It is a corporate growth strategy first and foremost; retention is more of a fringe benefit than a separate goal.

The emphasis in personal growth should be on the increased ability to meet the needs of the company's customers, not just the getting of a promotion or pay increase. Both of them are worthwhile objectives and should be serious human resource issues, but giving someone either is not a substitute for providing avenues for increased proficiency. Just as warm and fuzzy human resource policies are not a substitute for fair compensation and advancement opportunities, the careless proliferation of authority and swelling paychecks to buy loyalty only works briefly. The promotions and pay increases should recognize accomplishments and anticipate continued productivity.

The first step is some strategic thinking about the corporate goals and the skills necessary for long term sustained growth. Predicting the future becomes hazardous when we attempt to be too specific about events and circumstances, but wrong guesses about human proficiencies are seldom as critical as we might think. If we anticipate a need for C++ programmers, but the real shortage is in Java skills, we will find it easier to retrain C++ staffers in Java than to ramp up the data entry staff to Java programming or hire new persons to do the work.

The key is to promote a knowledge worker friendly culture. Some approaches are:

- Cite the development of skills and related training in recognizing employees; associate knowledge worker growth at every opportunity.

- Emphasize learning opportunities when recruiting; especially when advertising or posting jobs. If you highlight training as a corporate norm, you will attract the type of persons who have that attitude and reinforce the concept with current employees.

- Celebrate learning accomplishments of all varieties, even those not supported by or directly related to corporate goals. People who learn any topic are growth oriented, and their broad acceptance validates training as a personal goal.

- Use the company's long term goals and skill proficiency requirements to develop individual learning plans that correlate. Be specific about the kinds of new functions and responsibilities that you anticipate for the future.

- Incorporate career planning and knowledge worker concepts into the performance review process.

- Cite the knowledge development accomplishments in coordination with recognition of record of achievements in both creativity and productivity.

Beyond the development of a knowledge work environment and a personal growth culture, there is always an immediate need for on-the-job personal development. But that kind of progress is dubious if the job itself is poorly designed and unchallenging. Some of the factors to examine when reviewing job quality are:

- Is it a short cycle, highly repetitive job that has been mechanized in similar situations?

- Can you find inexpensive or cost effective software to perform many functions of the job?

- Was the job formerly held on a long-term basis by someone recently retired?

- Do other staff members simply save the work when the incumbent goes on vacation, and have it waiting for him or her when they return?

It is important to be aware of dead end jobs and to engineer increases in responsibilities and challenges. Good people have a low tolerance for intellectually stagnant jobs.

Of parallel significance, one of the intrinsic responsibilities of supervisors and managers is to plan for and encourage skill growth that will permit career growth for subordinates. As a part of the job design and skills inventory mentioned earlier, the alternative next steps in advancement should be identified and an individual growth plan constructed. Typically, the additional skills help staff to perform better in their current jobs as well as prepare them for future ones.

> ★ **The biggest barrier to growth is often the reluctance of supervisors to risk losing their more competent subordinates or fostering individuals whose career advancement is more rapid than their own.** ★

The biggest barrier to growth is often the reluctance of supervisors to risk losing their more competent subordinates or fostering individuals whose career advancement is more rapid than their own. More senior managers should be alert to this possibility and clarify their development duties.

When significant and immediate job skill growth is not practical, other resources should be considered:

- Company sponsored skill development courses at local community colleges or commercial training companies.

- Internal training operations that provide employees with opportunities to both develop new skills and to show off their own accomplishments. Cross training is very motivating when people who work together are sharing skills in formal and informal settings.

- Create specialized classes using outside experts to lead both short seminars and extended classroom studies.

- Where practical, underwrite correspondence courses and recognize successful accomplishments.

- Send both technical professionals and production line staff to trade shows and on customer site troubleshooting visits.

- Assign a variety of staff to development projects that enlarge their recognition of company functions and opportunities.

- Create a corporate university to consolidate and emphasize broad intellectual development.

- Honor mentor relationships and recognize individuals who help others grow and succeed; consider sponsoring and encouraging mentoring.

- Establish an internship program where your inside experts can test their skills and ability in transmitting them by working with young persons who want to grow.

The essence of a knowledge worker environment is to consistently honor intellectual growth whenever and wherever you find it.

Use both formal programs and the company's bully pulpit to recognize, encourage, and celebrate the desire to learn.

The talent powered company does sound too good to be true. But most experienced employees have enjoyed a taste of this kind of environment, however temporary. The ephemeral nature comes from the lack of commitment to the values explicit in a talent powered company. People will respond well to a special challenge when there is an obvious threat to the survival of a company or an outstanding opportunity presents itself. Management fails its responsibility and its potential when its lack of interest in persons, the people with talent, becomes evident later. With the crisis past or opportunities achieved, they anticipate a continued level of energy without a parallel leadership commitment.

As a solo function of the human resource department, retention efforts frequently fail. With exception of a select few, employees don't work for or with supervisors in human resources. The people who make a difference in the rest of the company are supervisors and managers; they represent the company to their subordinates and are a role model for them as well. The retention process needs to be widespread.

If retention is a problem for a given supervisor or manager, he or she can be a significant part of the solution. Some of the tactics that can work are:

- Maintain your accessibility to subordinates. In the press of getting work done and dealing with the myriad responsibilities of your job, keep your door and mind open to their questions, comments, and concerns.

- Listen when they do open up, recognizing that they could be more willing to talk to you seriously than you imagine.

- Create opportunities for information and idea exchanges to take place. Use a mix of open meetings and one-on-one conferences to attract communications to you.

- Explore the motivations of subordinates, finding out what they expect of their job, the company, peer colleagues, customers, and yourself. Discover their ambitions for the future and the accomplishments from the past that have special importance for them.

- Keep confidences. Don't share even the most casual revelation without checking for their approval, and avoid gossip of all kinds. When you start dropping insights about other people, the person with whom you are talking will assume that you will be cavalier about sharing things that they tell you in confidence.

- Model the ethics, attitudes, skills, and enthusiasms that you want subordinates to demonstrate. Be honest about your shortcomings and open about your ongoing efforts to correct them.

- Address issues as they occur whenever possible. Put differences out on the table and deal with them as fairly as you know how; conflicts left unresolved tend to fester and compromise accomplishments of every variety.

- Follow the old military adage—praise in public, criticize in private. If your praise is ill placed, your subordinates will probably attribute it to excess enthusiasm and forgive you. A private reprimand shows respect for the individual and allows a non-threatening exchange of viewpoints.

- Avoid blanket criticisms like the plague; they tend to hurt your best people without motivating the marginal employees. Irresponsible people assume you are talking about someone else anyway.

- Ask your subordinates for their input to resolving solutions, even when they seem to be overwhelmed. More often than not, they know what to do, but want your sanction to proceed and hope that you will concur with their judgment without their telling you what it is. Read the book, *The One Minute Manager*, for "how to" specifics.

- Applaud initiative. When someone resolves a tricky situation on their own, recognize both the good thinking and *the courage* to do the right thing without confirming their good judgment with you or others. Also, be tolerant of errors of enthusiasm because their choices will not always be correct. Amend the thinking, not the initiative.

- Model and share your decision-making processes. Take the mystery out of management, and represent good decisions as both possible and permissible for them to make.

- Tolerate and encourage the exchange of information and ideas. Your subordinates may be conspiring to undercut your authority and embarrass you with your boss, but it is much more likely that they are trying to get the work done right and on time. Encourage them to communicate with each other and parties outside your area of responsibility on routine matters, and only draw you into the communication process when a special problem or opportunity develops.

- Don't take yourself too seriously. Work on earning respect and reserve the authority you possess for the special situations when it is really needed. Display and allow a balanced sense of humor about the necessary travails of doing business.

- Support your staff. Any criticism they receive is an indictment of your guidance and leadership, and should come directly from you. Take any outside blame for their short-comings and address them positively, privately, and promptly.

- Make your expectations reasonable and clear. Whenever possible, label the different levels of possible performance as good, excellent, and outstanding. When the higher levels are achieved, recognize them specifically.

- Establish your own personal acclaim policy, even if you don't publish it—when to prepare a letter of commendation for the personnel file, when to cite performance in a company newsletter, when to recommend for a bonus or a raise, when to express a simple thank you or thumbs up. Use it not so much as a way to parcel out praise, but as a standard to drive your acknowledgment process. Praise is a management discipline that is too easy to neglect, and so productive to pursue. Distinguish yourself as one of those people who can recognize outstanding performance when they see it.

- Display achievement records. One of the most successful managers I have ever known had one wall of his office crowded with letters of commendation for his employees, special certificates, copies of their diplomas, the report cards of his children and theirs, letters of praise from customers, and charts of output achievements. His explanation to visitors was simple; "I am recognized for what they accomplish."

- Know your people. Find out what they take pride in, at work or away. What values do they honor and which people do they respect? Discover enough to introduce them at a banquet with words that no one would contradict and could make their mothers cry with pride. Also, take the plunge and tell them a little about yourself.

- Keep a record of the years of experience that your staff have within the company and the industry; make it a part of your published achievement records. Recognize the individual senior contributors to group success and cite the hallmarks of their growth in terms of personal skills and achievements as well as promotions and change of job responsibilities. Celebrate every five-year anniversary with a cake and custom T-shirt—as a bare minimum. Use those occasions to reiterate the difference that experience makes within your organization.

- Energize the staff with challenges, relax them with acknowledgments. Avoid the appearance of always ratcheting up performance requirements, but be diligent in sharing with them how competing companies or groups create a dynamic situation.

- Thoughtfully select mentors for new people. Ideally, as their new supervisor, you are their primary mentor, but have the insight to recognize that you will not be available each time they have a question and the person physically closest to them may not be the best source of guidance. Make the mentor task one of respect and acknowledgment, make the necessary temporary adjustments in job responsibilities to allow the mentor time to perform effectively, and cite the mentor accomplishments in pay increase recommendations and performance reviews.

- Delegate diligently. Nothing distinguishes a manager more than having a staff that can take care of all the routine and some of the non-routine responsibilities of the area with little input from their boss. The ideal manager mans the rudder, but does not row the boat. Good delegation develops staff skills, builds their self-esteem, increases teamwork, encourages effective communications, promotes cross training, and enhances staff self-esteem. Most importantly, good delegation gives the manager or supervisor the time and energy to lead effectively.

■ Sponsor changes that improve working conditions, work processes, equipment, software, and materials. Allow subordinates to take the lead on changes that are near and dear to them, but help however and whenever you can. At a bare minimum, don't get in the way. Often your biggest contribution can be in showing them the accepted or most effective way to make the changes.

■ Foster informal as well as formal teams. It can be as simple as, "Will you three look into that and get back to me with some ideas by the end of next week?" Encourage those working on related tasks to share data and insights with you *and* among themselves. Give some credit to those that take up the slack when one or more persons are away from their routine tasks on a special project.

■ Provide space and time for team meetings; be open-handed with resources at your disposal.

■ Respect the privacy of subordinates.

Most successful retention efforts are a combination of routine leadership and good manners. When staff, especially entry-level supervisors, fail to perform those functions, it is because they have not been modeled for them. The biggest challenge for senior management is not to train staff in talent powered processes, but to demonstrate and validate their application in the workplace.

# ABOUT THE AUTHORS

## John Lewis McCarter Jr.

John McCarter is a management consultant with broad experience in both human resources and industrial engineering. As a consultant with H. B. Maynard & Company, he worked with a broad variety of industrial concerns in productivity and labor incentive development, performing wage surveys and job evaluations for various clients. He also served as Senior Instructor at the Maynard Management Institute and taught hundreds of engineers and other management professionals work measurement technology. Clients included Wean United, Oklahoma Gas & Electric, Smith and Wesson, and Masland Carpet. He is a qualified instructor in all the Maynard Operations Sequence Techniques (MOST) systems.

At Charles Brooks Associates, John developed extensive operations training programs for the banking and automotive industries, and worked with Service Dimensions Inc. as well. Leading banking clients include Chemical Bank, NationsBank (now Bank of America), First American, and Manufacturers Hanover Bank. Industrial clients are General Motors and Siemens Automotive.

John McCarter is a team oriented professional, providing active leadership of client teams to accomplish challenging goals on time while developing the technical and management capacities of team members. He is an innovator in the creating of incentive programs for traditionally non-incentive jobs and an insightful organizer of job duties and responsibilities. John is also an outplacement special-

**111**

ist and a co-author of *The Employers' Guide to Recruiting on the Internet* and *The Best 100 Web Sites for HR Professionals.*

He is a native of the Carolinas, a graduate of Clemson University, and the Belk College of Business, University of North Carolina at Charlotte. A long time resident of Charlotte, he is an avid reader and student of politics. He can be reached via email at: career@bellsouth.net.

## Ray Schreyer

Ray Schreyer is currently Director of Employment for Little & Associates in Charlotte, NC. He has over 20 years of experience in Human Resources, Staffing, and Change Management. Significant employers have included such firms as Union Carbide, Union Oil Company, BASF, and First Union National Bank. He was one of the first individuals in America to recognize the significant impact of internet recruiting and served as a content provider to America Online's Career Center and as the Director of New Business for Monster.com in the mid 90's.

Ray received his masters training in Industrial/Organizational Psychology from the University of North Carolina. He is co-author of *The Employer's Guide to Recruiting On the Internet* and *The Best 100 Web Sites for HR Professionals.* A native of Chicago, he migrated to the Carolinas in the mid 80's and fell in love with the hospitality and lifestyle of the community. He currently resides in Matthews, North Carolina with his wife Gayle. Ray can be reached via email at: nccareer@aol.com.

# INDEX

# BUSINESS AND CAREER RESOURCES

Contact Impact Publications for a free annotated listing of resources or visit the World Wide Web for a complete listing of resources: www.impactpublications.com. The following books are available directly from Impact Publications. Complete the following form or list the titles, include postage (see formula at the end), enclose payment, and send your order to:

**IMPACT PUBLICATIONS**
9104 Manassas Drive, Suite N
Manassas Park, VA  20111-5211
Tel 1-800/361-1055, 703/361-7300, or Fax 703/335-9486
Quick and easy online ordering: *www.impactpublications.com*

| Qty. | Titles | Price | Total |
|------|--------|-------|-------|
| **OTHER BOOKS BY JOHN McCARTER AND RAY SCHREYER** | | | |
| _____ | The Best 100 Web Sites for HR Professionals | 12.95 | _____ |
| _____ | The Employer's Guide to Recruiting on the Internet | 24.95 | _____ |
| **THE CAREERSAVVY SERIES** | | | |
| _____ | 100 Top Internet Job Sites | 12.95 | _____ |
| _____ | 101 Hiring Mistakes Employers Make…Avoid Them | 14.95 | _____ |
| _____ | The Best 100 Web Sites for HR Professionals | 12.95 | _____ |
| _____ | The Difficult Hire | 14.95 | _____ |
| _____ | Savvy Interviewing | 10.95 | _____ |
| _____ | The Savvy Resume Writer | 12.95 | _____ |
| **HIRING & RETENTION** | | | |
| _____ | 45 Effective Ways for Hiring Smart! | 24.95 | _____ |
| _____ | 96 Great Interview Questions to Ask Before You Hire | 16.95 | _____ |
| _____ | Ask the Right Questions, Hire the Best People | 14.99 | _____ |
| _____ | CareerXroads 2000 | 26.95 | _____ |
| _____ | Complete Reference Checking Handbook | 29.95 | _____ |
| _____ | Directory of Executive Recruiters 2000 | 44.95 | _____ |
| _____ | Employer's Guide to Recruiting on the Internet | 24.95 | _____ |
| _____ | Essential Book of Interviewing | 15.00 | _____ |
| _____ | Fast Forward MBA in Hiring | 14.95 | _____ |
| _____ | Finding and Keeping Great Employees | 24.95 | _____ |
| _____ | High Impact Hiring | 34.95 | _____ |
| _____ | Hire With Your Head | 29.95 | _____ |
| _____ | Hiring: How to Find & Keep the Best People | 12.99 | _____ |
| _____ | Hiring and Managing Personnel Library | 299.95 | _____ |
| _____ | Love 'Em or Lose 'Em | 17.95 | _____ |
| _____ | Manager's Book of Questions | 12.95 | _____ |
| _____ | Smart Hiring | 12.95 | _____ |
| _____ | Smart Staffing | 19.95 | _____ |

| Qty. | Titles | Price | Total |
|------|--------|-------|-------|
| _____ | Unofficial Guide to Hiring & Firing Employees | 16.00 | _____ |
| _____ | Verify Those Credentials | 19.95 | _____ |
| _____ | Weddle's Guide to Employment Web-sites | 21.95 | _____ |

## MOTIVATING & ENERGIZING YOUR WORKFORCE

| | | | |
|------|--------|-------|-------|
| _____ | 1001 Ways to Energize Employees | 12.00 | _____ |
| _____ | 1001 Ways to Reward Employees | 12.00 | _____ |
| _____ | A New Attitude | 99.00 | _____ |
| _____ | Attitude! | 149.00 | _____ |
| _____ | Bringing Out the Best in People | 21.95 | _____ |
| _____ | Dilbert Principle | 20.00 | _____ |
| _____ | Getting Employees to Fall in Love with Your Company | 17.95 | _____ |
| _____ | How to Be a Star at Work | 12.00 | _____ |
| _____ | Joy of Work | 22.00 | _____ |
| _____ | Motivating and Rewarding Employees | 99.00 | _____ |
| _____ | Motivation and Goal-Setting | 99.00 | _____ |
| _____ | Passionate Organization | 24.95 | _____ |
| _____ | Take This Job and Thrive | 14.95 | _____ |

## RESUMES & LETTERS

| | | | |
|------|--------|-------|-------|
| _____ | 100 Winning Resumes for $100,000+ Jobs | 24.95 | _____ |
| _____ | 101 Quick Tips for a Dynamite Resume | 13.95 | _____ |
| _____ | 201 Winning Cover Letters for the $100,000+ Jobs | 24.95 | _____ |
| _____ | 1500+ Key Words for 100,000+ | 14.95 | _____ |
| _____ | Dynamite Cover Letters | 14.95 | _____ |
| _____ | Dynamite Resumes | 14.95 | _____ |
| _____ | Haldane's Best Cover Letters for Professionals | 15.95 | _____ |
| _____ | Haldane's Best Resumes for Professionals | 15.95 | _____ |
| _____ | High Impact Resumes and Letters | 19.95 | _____ |
| _____ | Sure-Hire Resumes | 14.95 | _____ |
| _____ | Winning Resumes | 10.95 | _____ |

## INTERVIEWING: JOBSEEKERS

| | | | |
|------|--------|-------|-------|
| _____ | 101 Dynamite Answers to Interview Questions | 12.95 | _____ |
| _____ | 101 Dynamite Questions to Ask at Your Job Interview | 14.95 | _____ |
| _____ | 101 Tough Interview Questions. . . | 14.95 | _____ |
| _____ | 111 Dynamite Ways to Ace Your Job Interview | 13.95 | _____ |
| _____ | Haldane's Best Answers to Tough Interview Questions | 15.95 | _____ |
| _____ | Interview for Success | 15.95 | _____ |
| _____ | Savvy Interviewing | 10.95 | _____ |

## NETWORKING AND JOB SEARCHING TOOLS

| | | | |
|------|--------|-------|-------|
| _____ | 100 Top Internet Job Sites | 12.95 | _____ |
| _____ | Dynamite Networking for Dynamite Jobs | 15.95 | _____ |
| _____ | Dynamite Tele-Search | 12.95 | _____ |
| _____ | Electronic Resumes | 19.95 | _____ |
| _____ | Internet Resumes | 14.95 | _____ |

## SALARY NEGOTIATIONS

| | | | |
|------|--------|-------|-------|
| _____ | Dynamite Salary Negotiations | 15.95 | _____ |
| _____ | Get a Raise in 7 Days | 14.95 | _____ |
| _____ | Get More Money on Your Next Job | 14.95 | _____ |
| _____ | Negotiate Your Job Offer | 14.95 | _____ |

| Qty. | Titles | Price | Total |
|------|--------|-------|-------|

## IMAGE, ETIQUETTE, & COMMUNICATION

| Qty. | Titles | Price | Total |
|------|--------|-------|-------|
| _____ | 101 Secrets of Highly Effective Speakers | 14.95 | _____ |
| _____ | Dressing Smart in the New Millennium | 13.95 | _____ |
| _____ | John Malloy's Dress for Success (For Men) | 13.99 | _____ |
| _____ | New Women's Dress for Success | 12.99 | _____ |
| _____ | Red Socks Don't Work | 14.95 | _____ |
| _____ | You've Only Got 3 Seconds | 22.95 | _____ |

## INSPIRATION & EMPOWERMENT

| Qty. | Titles | Price | Total |
|------|--------|-------|-------|
| _____ | Beating Job Burnout | 12.95 | _____ |
| _____ | Big Things Happen When You Do the Little Things Right | 15.00 | _____ |
| _____ | Chicken Soup for the Soul Series | 87.95 | _____ |
| _____ | Do What You Love, the Money Will Follow | 11.95 | _____ |
| _____ | Get What You Deserve | 23.00 | _____ |
| _____ | If Life Is A Game, These Are the Rules | 15.00 | _____ |
| _____ | Seven Habits of Highly Effective People | 14.00 | _____ |

☞ **SUBTOTAL**      $ _____

☞ Virginia residents add 4½% sales tax)      _____

☞ Shipping/handling, Continental U.S., $5.00 +      _____ $5.00
plus following percentages when **SUBTOTAL** is:

    ☐ $30-$100—multiply SUBTOTAL by 8%      _____

    ☐ $100-$999—multiply SUBTOTAL by 7%      _____

    ☐ $1,000-$4,999—multiply SUBTOTAL by 6%      _____

    ☐ Over $5,000—multiply SUBTOTAL by 5%      _____

☞    ☐ If shipped outside Continental US, add another 5%      _____

☞ **TOTAL ENCLOSED**      $ _____

**SHIP TO:** (street address only for UPS or RPS delivery)

Name _____

Address _____

_____

_____

Telephone _____

I enclose ☐ Check ☐ Money Order in the amount of: $ _____

Charge $_____ to ☐ Visa ☐ MC ☐ AmEx

Card # _____ Exp: _____ / _____

Signature _____

# DISCOVER HUNDREDS OF ADDITIONAL RESOURCES ON THE WORLD WIDE WEB!

Looking for the newest and best books, directories, newsletters, wall charts, training programs, videos, computer software, and kits to help you energize your employees, effectively address sexual harassment issues, or improve your networking skills? Want to learn the most effective way to find a job in Asia or relocate to San Francisco? Are you curious about how to recruit a new employee using the Internet or about what you'll be doing five years from now? Are you trying to keep up-to-date on the latest HR resources, but are not able to find the latest catalogs, brochures, or newsletters on today's "best of the best" resources?

Welcome to the first virtual career bookstore on the Internet. Now you're only a click away with Impact Publications' electronic solution to the resource challenge. Visit this rich site to quickly discover everything you ever wanted to know about workplace diversity, career development, and compensation and benefits—including many useful resources that are difficult to find in local bookstores and libraries. The site also includes what's new and hot, tips for job search success, and monthly specials. Check it out today!

*www.impactpublications.com*